O9-AIF-722

AMERICA
AFTER
VIETNAM

EDWARD F. DOLAN

AMERICA AFTER VIETNAM

LEGACIES OF A HATED WAR

89-174
Chapt. II

Franklin Watts / 1989
New York / London / Toronto / Sydney

Photographs courtesy of:
Gamma/Liaison: pp. 24, 88, 119 (Sattleberger),
123, 141 (Jean Claude Labbe); UPI/Bettmann: pp. 31, 37, 41, 49 (both),
55, 67, 72, 81, 99; U.S. Military Academy, West Point: p. 133.

CONTENTS

AMERICA AFTER VIETNAM

INTRODUCTION

The word *legacy* means "gift." Ordinarily, the idea of a gift is a happy one for both the giver and the recipient, and so it may seem odd to use the word in connection with a war. But there is no question that every war ever fought has left behind its legacies for the peoples who fought it.

Most legacies of war are dreadful to behold. To name just one, Germany's terrible "gift" from World War II was to be left in total ruins and in deep shame for having permitted the emergence of the cruel regime responsible for triggering the global conflict that killed millions of people.

But some legacies of war, though born in horror, must be seen as beneficial. For example, humans have traveled into space, have walked on the moon, and have built the craft that are now probing ever deeper into the far reaches of the universe because of the developments in rocketry in World War II.

Many Americans look on the Vietnam War as the most hated conflict in United States history (others think the Civil War to have been even more detested). This is because, unlike World Wars I and II and the Korean War, the Vietnam conflict came to be opposed by vast segments of the American public and caused a divisiveness that threatened to rip the nation apart. In the giving of legacies, however, it was no different than any other war. It left to the people of the United States and Vietnam a variety of legacies, which remain with us today. Some are tragic, and some, although born in horror, promise benefits for the people of both countries.

One of the most tragic of these legacies took shape when the United States "bombed" South Vietnam with some 17 million gallons of the herbicide Agent Orange during the 1960s.[1] The herbicide was used to strip away the jungle foliage that provided such excellent cover for attacks by enemy guerrilla forces. In recent years, thousands of American veterans and Vietnamese citizens have contracted illnesses, some of them deadly, that are suspected to be the results of having been exposed to Agent Orange.

And what of a legacy that has risen out of horrors of battle and air bombings to show itself to be a benefit? As a result of the war and the upheavals that followed it, countless people fled Indochina (Vietnam and neighboring Laos and Cambodia). Thousands made their way to the United States. Here, although some met with difficulties in the communities in which they settled, they have made new, happy, and successful lives for themselves. Here, they have contributed much to the social, ethnic, and economic fabric of American life.

There is not enough space in this book, or perhaps in any book, to talk at length about all the legacies left by the Vietnam War. Consequently, we are going to limit ourselves to five that are considered extremely important because they have very directly touched the lives of Americans everywhere, including perhaps you. They are legacies with which we all may have to live for the rest of our lives.

Because this book is being written for an American audience, these legacies are five that have been bequeathed especially to the United States. Others of a quite different sort have been left to Vietnam. But, though we'll be concentrating on the United States, we'll find that these legacies likewise touch the Vietnamese people deeply. In the course of the book, we'll also come upon other legacies left by the war. We'll pause briefly to discuss them.

What are these five legacies? The first three concern the Americans who served in the war:

The cold welcome given the service people when they returned from the war. It was a distressing welcome that stemmed from the deep hatred felt by millions of Americans for the war and the way the fighting ended. It alienated many returning veterans from their fellow citizens and made them wonder if they would ever again fit into the mainstream of their nation's life. One veteran spoke for many when he said, "I went to Vietnam thinking I was a good American who was doing my duty for my country. I came back and ended up feeling like a criminal."

The invisible wounds—the psychological and emotional damages suffered by many veterans because of the nature and viciousness of the war.

The harm believed to have been suffered by the thousands of U.S. service people who were exposed to the herbicide Agent Orange. It is a legacy that has reached out to touch their spouses and children.

The fourth legacy turns from the veterans themselves and looks to:

The anguish suffered by the families of the U.S. service and civilian personnel who went to Vietnam and were never seen again—the men and women who were listed as missing in action (MIA). The quest to find these missing Americans, both living and dead, and bring them home has occupied the American mind and troubled the American conscience ever since the war's end.

The fifth legacy:

The problems faced by the many Indochinese refugees who have come to the United States and by the Americans in whose communities they have settled to build new lives for themselves and begin making their contributions to the nation's society.

/ 11 /

This book is being written with the hope that, in learning of the five legacies, all of us will gain a deeper insight into what the Vietnam War did to our nation. The war left the United States deeply wounded and divided, and caused many Americans to lose faith in their country. Those wounds are now healing. There is a returning pride and faith in our country. Perhaps this book will help us see how far the healing process has come and how far it still has to go. To assist in the healing, while never forgetting the source of the harm, is the duty of every one of us.

CHAPTER

ONE

THE HATED WAR

The Vietnam War has been called

The most hated conflict in United States history (with the possible exception of the Civil War). It split the American public into two sharply opposed camps. On the one side were all the people who supported the nation's participation in the fighting; on the other were those who not only opposed the U.S. role in Vietnam but also hated the thought of any war. The split led to such tragedies as rioting in the streets and a widespread sense that the country had lost the ideals that had made it great.

The first war not won by the United States. A peace treaty in 1973 was supposed to end the fighting. But it served no such purpose. The Americans and the North Vietnamese accused each other of violating the terms of the treaty, and the struggle raged on until the North Vietnamese won a final victory in 1975. As many Americans saw things, the treaty did nothing but end the U.S. role in the war and allow the country to withdraw from the fighting. The sense of shame that they felt made the war all the more hated.

One of the costliest wars, in both life and money, ever waged by the U.S. The nation spent $150 billion on the conflict, put 8.7 million Americans into uniform between 1965 and 1973 (the years of our greatest involvement), and sent 3.4 million of their number to Vietnam, where some 58,000 lost their lives and 300,000 were wounded.[1]

This war left in its wake many sad legacies for both the American and Vietnamese people. They are gifts that have affected the quality of life in both countries through all the years since the fighting ended.

Whether these legacies are terrible or beneficial, they have touched all of us and may well continue to touch us for as long as we live. But before we can speak of them with any real understanding, we need to know the history of the war that left them to us.

THE ROOTS OF
THE VIETNAM WAR

With a coastline that stretches for more than 1,000 miles down the western edge of the South China Sea, Vietnam is a long, narrow country of 128,402 square miles. It is divided between rugged mountains and fertile deltas and is rich in agricultural lands, forests, and mineral deposits. Its immediate neighbors are China to the northwest and Laos and Cambodia (Kampuchea) to the west.

The roots of the Vietnam War can be traced to the years just before World War II.[2] At that time, the people of Vietnam were a diverse lot. Included in their number were not only the Vietnamese themselves but also many Chinese, Laotians, Cambodians, and Thais. Socially, they ranged from primitive tribesmen to the wealthiest of merchants. The nation's religions were just as diverse; the people worshiped as Roman Catholics, Protestants, Buddhists, and Confucians. Despite this diversity, most of the people shared a single ambition. They wanted to be free of foreign domination. They wanted Vietnam to be an independent nation.

The foreign country under whose control they lived was France. The French had invaded Vietnam in the mid-nineteenth

/ 14 /

century and had then rounded out their conquest with the subjugation of neighboring Laos and Cambodia. Together, the three holdings, all rich in natural resources, became known as French Indochina. Today, they are known simply as Indochina.

Throughout the years leading up to World War II, the people of Vietnam constantly agitated for independence from France. But their every effort failed because they lacked a single nationalist organization. Rather, they were divided into small revolutionary groups and movements that were built along religious, political, and socioeconomic lines. Some groups, for example, were made up of Buddhists, while others were manned by farmers, and still others by communists.

Soon after World War II erupted in distant Europe, one of these groups managed to become the strongest of the lot: the *Viet Nam Doc Lap Dong Minh,* or the Vietnam League for Independence. Popularly known as the Viet Minh, it took shape when several communist and noncommunist groups in the country's northern area joined forces for greater strength. Despite its noncommunist factions, the Viet Minh's leadership was principally communist. At its head was a longtime disciple of Marxism, Ho Chi Minh.

Ho Chi Minh
and the Viet Minh

Born in 1890 and dedicated to revolutionary politics from an early age, Ho Chi Minh spent his young manhood in Europe, first in Paris and then in Moscow, where he was trained as a communist agent. On returning to Asia, he set up headquarters in Hong Kong and began to organize a number of pro-communist and anti-French activities in Indochina. When France fell to Germany in the first days of World War II, Ho shifted his headquarters to Vietnam and formed the Viet Minh.

The fall of France resulted in the loss of French prestige in Vietnam. In that loss, Ho saw a great opportunity to win his country's independence. It was to seize this opportunity that he formed the Viet Minh. Immediately, he set its forces to harassing the French businessmen, planters, and troops in Vietnam. Then,

/ 15 /

when Japanese troops arrived in the country as part of their nation's conquest of Asia, the Viet Minh quickly began to give them battle.

After the Japanese attack at Pearl Harbor thrust the United States into the war, the American armed forces mounted an assault that sent them moving northward through the Pacific from Guadalcanal to the island of Formosa, just below Japan itself. The assault also sent U.S. troops onto the Chinese mainland to face the Japanese there. Once in China, the U.S. realized that the country was highly vulnerable to a Japanese attack from neighboring Vietnam. This realization brought the Americans into contact with Ho Chi Minh and marked the beginning of an involvement with Vietnam that would last for years and lead to that most hated of wars.

Although the United States did not like the Viet Minh because of its communist leadership, it could not overlook what Ho and his people were doing to make life miserable for the Japanese. Consequently, to keep tabs on a possible attack out of Vietnam, the U.S. turned to Ho for help and offered him funds and arms in trade for intelligence information on Japan's activities.

Seven Turbulent Years

At war's end, French influence in Vietnam was greatly weakened. Ho moved quickly to take power. He declared the country an independent nation and established a government at the northern city of Hanoi. Despite his power, however, his actual authority was limited because he held sway only in the north. Southern Vietnam was dominated by nationalist groups formed chiefly along religious lines. Because these groups were sharply opposed to each other, the political scene in the south was a chaotic one that promised nothing but trouble in the future. And so, at the urging of a number of southern political figures who admired his leadership, Ho formed a provisional government that was meant to bind the north and south together. This provisional government was to supervise the two areas until a single, unified Vietnam could be established.

Since he had helped the Americans during the war, Ho had reason to hope that the U.S. would throw its support behind his government. But he was in for a disappointment. All U.S. support went instead to France, which was given back its Indochina holdings by the Allied powers. The United States, although traditionally opposed to colonial expansion, supported the French because of the fear that, unless they were in power there, the entire country would end up under Ho and his communist group.

French efforts to regain control of Vietnam resulted in seven years of bloody warfare. Ho's Viet Minh fought an unending guerrilla action. His fighters attacked or sabotaged French plantations, business establishments, and military installations. In 1954, the Viet Minh finally emerged as a conventional field army and attacked the great French fortification at Dien Bien Phu near the Laotian border. For two months, 40,000 Ho troops laid siege to the fortification before attacking it directly on May 7. They swarmed over the battered defenses, took 16,000 French troops prisoner, and ended France's hold on Vietnam.

The Divided Country

With the French defeat, one problem was ended, but another remained. Politically, the northern and southern areas were still sharply divided. Ho's communist Viet Minh held the north, while factions that were principally noncommunist had come to dominate in the south. How could Vietnam ever become a single, unified nation?

In 1954, that question went before an international conference held in Switzerland. The main purpose of the meeting—which was attended by representatives from Great Britain, the Soviet Union, the United States, France, and Vietnam—was to develop an armistice agreement between the French and the Vietnamese. But it also hammered out what seemed to be a simple answer to the question.

The country was to be temporarily divided into two states— North and South Vietnam. The division was to be made along a line roughly approximating the 17th parallel. For the time being, Ho would remain in power north of the line, and the anti-communist leader, Ngo Dinh Diem, would head the government south of the line. At the end of two years, an election would be held to unify the entire nation. The people on each side of the line would vote into power the government they preferred.

The solution may have been a simple one, but it posed a

problem for the United States. Ho Chi Minh was such a popular and respected figure in his homeland that the people in both North and South Vietnam called him by the affectionate nickname "Uncle Ho." The U.S. feared that, when the unification election took place, they would vote him into power, with the new nation becoming a communist state.

And so the United States threw its support behind Ngo Dinh Diem's South Vietnam. Diem was a longtime advocate of Vietnamese independence whose views were not only anti-communistic but strongly pro-American as well. The U.S. support was intended to help him develop a prosperous state that would attract more voters than Ho's government when the unification election was finally held.

The initial American support was principally economic. Between 1955 and 1962, the U.S. supplied South Vietnam with $2 billion in aid, a portion of which was earmarked for military aid, while $1.4 billion went to agricultural projects, among them programs intended to increase crop yields. Additionally, the U.S. assigned military advisors—685 in the beginning—to assist in the training of the South Vietnamese army.

American Disenchantment

The passing years, however, saw the United States become disenchanted with Diem. He revealed himself to be anything but a democratic leader. He stood accused of executing his political enemies by the hundreds and imprisoning them by the thousands. There were reports that he and his closest allies were cornering much of the U.S. aid and personally profiting from it. Although Diem was recognized as heading a corrupt regime, the American support continued. The U.S. commitment to build a South Vietnam stronger than a communist North Vietnam overrode all other considerations.

The situation in the South became so intolerable that, in 1955, a group of influential Vietnamese politicians, religious leaders, and military men demanded Diem's resignation. He countered by calling for a general election in South Vietnam and placing himself on the ballot as a candidate for president. On the surface, this appeared to be a democratic move: let the people themselves decide whether he would be ousted or allowed to remain at the head of the government. Behind the scenes, so the reports of the day went, Diem rigged the election in his favor by coercing the voters and suppressing the opposition candidates.

As expected, Diem won the election. On assuming the presidency in October 1955, he renamed the country the Republic of South Vietnam. He then canceled the upcoming unification election and said that South Vietnam would carry on as a nation independent of the north.

THE VIETNAM WAR

The Diem announcement outraged Ho Chi Minh's government in the North, and his many communist supporters in the South were outraged by Diem's announcement. Many of Ho's supporters in the South were banded together in an army of guerrilla fighters called the *Viet Cong San,* or the Vietnamese Communists, and known simply as the Vietcong. Ever since 1954, the Vietcong had sought to bring as much of the South as possible under their control so that the people there would vote for Ho's government in the unification election. Now, with Ho's approval, they set out to wrest the country from Diem's hands, doing so with a campaign of terror that saw them assassinate village chieftains, attack military installations, and sabotage plantations and industrial facilities.

That the campaign, which was waged with military supplies from the Soviet Union, succeeded and that the South Vietnamese army was incapable of stopping it could be plainly seen in the fact that the Vietcong guerrillas were soon dominating long stretches of the South's coastline and much of the country's rich delta land. By 1964, some 74 percent of South Vietnam was in Vietcong hands.

The American people watched the situation with growing frustration. They could see that South Vietnam was failing to become the successful democratic nation that the U.S. had envisioned. Not only was it headed by a corrupt government (Diem was assassinated in 1963, but the leaders who replaced him were proving to be equally corrupt), but its American-equipped army

/ 19 /

was showing itself helpless to fend off a band of guerrilla fighters who dressed not in uniforms but in the tattered clothing of the Vietnamese peasant.

Still, the U.S. determination to stall the advance of communism in Vietnam remained. American military and economic aid mounted steadily. By the end of 1961, the original force of 685 U.S. military advisors in Vietnam had risen to 2,000. In early 1962, 5,000 Americans were on Vietnamese duty; their number jumped to 11,000 by year's end. Ten months later, in November 1963, the total stood at 16,500. Throughout this period, the communist side of the struggle was carried out principally by the Vietcong. It was not until 1964 that Ho Chi Minh began to commit North Vietnamese army troops in appreciable numbers.

A Critical Year

Nineteen sixty-four was a critical year for the United States. It was the year that recorded two alleged attacks on the U.S. destroyer *Maddox* while the ship was patrolling the Gulf of Tonkin off the North Vietnamese coast. On both occasions, the attackers were PT boats, which were reported to have fired torpedoes at the ship. The fire was returned and three PT boats were sunk in the first of the engagements. On neither occasion was the destroyer struck or otherwise damaged.

The Ho government justified the attacks by charging that the American vessel had been participating in a South Vietnamese naval action along the North Vietnamese coast. The American government insisted that the ship had been on routine patrol and that it had been too far out at sea to have taken part in a coastal action. An angry President Lyndon B. Johnson went before Congress and asked for the authority to intensify U.S. military action in Vietnam. He worded his request in a resolution that became known as the Gulf of Tonkin Resolution.

Congress approved the resolution. From the moment of approval, the American involvement in Vietnam quickly deepened. The U.S. Air Force launched a long series of bombing attacks against North Vietnam and the enemy fighters in South Vietnam. Increasing numbers of men were dispatched across the Pacific. By the end of 1965, U.S. troop strength in South Vietnam stood at over 184,000; it rose to more than 385,000 in 1966 and to upwards of 475,000 in 1967. The total peaked at over 543,000 in early 1969.

The Growing Opposition

From its very beginning, the war divided American public opinion into two camps. On the one hand, there were many people who supported the nation's involvement and felt that communism should be fought wherever it was found. On the other, there were many who opposed the involvement. They argued that the United States was supporting a corrupt South Vietnamese regime in a revolutionary struggle that was not our business.

The first real opposition came from the nation's youth. Since the war was being fought mainly by men who were being conscripted into the military, the young people began by staging peace demonstrations, burning their draft cards, and refusing to answer the call to service. Some went to jail for their resistance. Others hid, sometimes alone in the woods, sometimes with companions in rural communes, sometimes in the homes of friends. Others fled the country, traveling to Mexico, Canada, and such European countries as England and Sweden. An estimated 30,000 to 60,000, for example, went to Canada.*

---

*Mention of the young men who refused to be drafted into the service brings us to another legacy of the war. For several years after the fighting ended, the U.S. was torn by controversy over what to do about them. Because the men had broken the law in evading the draft, many people argued that they should be punished. Just as many others felt that the men should be pardoned because they had followed their consciences in refusing to participate in a hated and useless war. President Jimmy Carter attempted to settle the issue in 1977 when he declared amnesty for most of the men. Amnesty is the procedure by which nations or organizations officially "forget" and dismiss certain offenses; the offenses are frequently of a political nature. In general, Mr. Carter's action put an end to the legacy of controversy. But many men who had fled to foreign nations refused to come home. Some feared that, despite the President's amnesty, they would still be punished. Others remained abroad because they had built lives for themselves in their new homelands and were content to stay where they were. Many have never returned to the U.S.

As time went on and the involvement deepened, the anti-war sentiment spread beyond the young people to greater and greater segments of the population. It took many forms.

There was shock at the heavy air strikes against the enemy in both the North and South, attacks that were seen as vicious. There was a growing nervousness when the fighting spread to Laos and Cambodia, where North Vietnamese–backed factions were trying to dislodge governments supported by the U.S. There was a sick feeling whenever the numbers of dead and wounded U.S. personnel were announced; everywhere it was heard that too many young Americans were being sacrificed to protect a corrupt regime. There was the same sick feeling at the number of Vietnamese citizens being maimed and killed by the U.S. air and ground forces; many people realized that the civilian garb worn by the Vietcong made it impossible for an infantryman to distinguish between an enemy guerrilla and an innocent civilian when protecting himself, but they still hated the killing.

In time, the belief took shape that the United States was being defeated. Despite the "body counts" of enemy dead issued by the military, both the Vietcong and the North Vietnamese remained strong. Attesting to their strength was the major attack they launched in 1968. Called the Tet offensive because it took place at the time of an annual Asian holiday, it struck at some thirty towns and cities in South Vietnam. Although the offensive ended in defeat for the attackers, it left no doubt that the enemy was capable of fighting a long war.

The feeling that the United States was losing brought a sense of shame to many Americans. In others, it triggered two suspicions—that the military was lying in its enemy body counts and that the U.S. leadership was defying the growing anti-war sentiment at home and pursuing a lost cause out of sheer stubbornness. Hadn't President Johnson said that he was determined not to be the first president to preside over an American defeat? The remark struck countless people as a terrible example of false pride.

In all, great segments of the American public came to feel a deep sense of guilt, shame, and frustration over the nation's in-

/ 22 /

volvement in Vietnam and its reluctance to disentangle itself. It seemed to them that the country had somehow lost the ideals that had made it great.

The Last Years

The anti-war sentiment reached its zenith—and began to bear fruit—in 1968. In that year, police battled with peace demonstrators who gathered outside the Democratic National Convention in Chicago. President Lyndon Johnson announced that, in great part to help restore peace in the country, he would not seek re-election to the presidency. Talks to end the war began in Paris between the United States and North Vietnam. Presidential candidate Richard M. Nixon vowed that he would end the conflict if elected.

On taking office in 1969, Mr. Nixon embarked on a policy that he called "Vietnamization." He said that it was aimed at building the South Vietnamese army to the point where it could defend its country by itself, without any outside help. The President then began withdrawing U.S. troops from Southeast Asia. By 1971, the South Vietnamese had assumed the main responsibility for the ground fighting. The United States continued to provide them with air support and economic aid.

The peace talks at Paris, often stalled by angry disagreements, continued until 1973. In January of that year, a treaty was finally signed. It called for the end of the fighting and the withdrawal of all American troops, along with the troops of the other nations that had assisted South Vietnam, among them Australia. All of the United States forces were on their way home two months after the signing.

But the treaty did not end the struggle. The North Vietnamese army and the Vietcong continued to attack in the South, their aim being to conquer the capital city of Saigon. The attack ended in success for them on April 30, 1975, when Saigon fell after a long siege. At last—but not in the way the United States had anticipated—Vietnam was reunified. The reunification was formalized in 1976 and the entire country was named the Socialist Republic of Vietnam.

Although the legacies left by the war have touched us all, the Americans who have been most deeply touched are the nation's veterans—those who served in Vietnam. It is to their legacies that we now turn to understand how they affected the veterans and to see how many they touched, how painful was their touch, and how successfully or unsuccessfully the veterans have managed to survive in their presence.

North Vietnamese troops march through the streets of Saigon on April 30, 1975

THE FIRST LEGACY

THE COLD WELCOME HOME

CHAPTER
TWO
WELCOME
TO ALIENATION

When the time came for U.S. servicemen to return home, the Vietnam War differed in three ways from the other conflicts that marked the twentieth century—World War I, World War II, and the Korean War. These differences made the return of the Vietnam veterans a difficult, sometimes shattering one that left many feeling alienated from their country for years to come.[1]

First, the Americans who fought in the earlier wars returned home as victors. Both World Wars I and II ended in total defeat for the enemy. The Korean fighting came to a close with a truce that paved the way to peace talks between North Korea and the United Nations forces, of which the United States was a member. And so the men came back from these wars as heroes and were greeted as such by a grateful public.

Second, they were greeted warmly because they had fought in wars that had the support of most, if not all, of their countrymen. This was particularly true of World War II, when the nation fully recognized that its troops in Europe were fighting the evil represented by Hitler's Nazi Germany, while the men in the Pacific were

/ 29 /

battling the enemy who had attacked the U.S. without warning at Pearl Harbor.

Finally, especially in the two world wars, most of the men did not return until the fighting had ended. When they finally did return, most came home with their units. The units were greeted with ceremonies of welcome and by cheering throngs. Often, the men then marched in victory parades, sometimes in the nation's great cities and sometimes in its smallest hometowns, while an appreciative public showered them with ticker tape, confetti, even flowers.

But what of the Vietnam veterans? Their experience was quite different. To begin with, they did not return en masse at the end of the fighting. Rather, they came home throughout the course of the war after having served a tour of duty, a period that usually lasted a year. Nor did they return with their units. Instead, on completing their tours, they were replaced by others and shipped home alone or in small groups.

And so, there was little or no chance for an organized welcome by the government or by the Americans who supported the country's role in the fighting. Then, when the men did return in greater numbers after the signing of the Paris peace pact in 1973, the country was exhausted from years of living with the divisiveness, anger, shame, and guilt that the conflict had triggered. Hardly anyone seemed in the mood for a hero's welcome. The veterans returned to a cold, silent, and, as we'll see, often angry reception.

It was a reception that left many feeling alienated from their country, feeling as if they were strangers in their own hometowns. They seemed to have come home as misfits who had no place in the mainstream of the nation's life. They wondered if they would ever win—or ever want to win—a place for themselves in the United States.

On March 7, 1985, ten years after the Vietnam War ended, Vietnam veterans marched up Broadway in New York City in their first welcome-home parade.

WELCOME HOME

The silence and coldness could not help but hurt. Happily, the pain was eased for many men by the loving welcomes extended by friends and families. But it was worsened by the anger that the war had generated. The men ran into a phenomenon that made no sense to them. They learned that many Americans were taking out their feelings on the veterans and blaming them personally for the war and how it had ended.[2]

The men came face-to-face with this view in encounters with strangers, friends, and relatives alike. What happened during these meetings depended on whether a veteran ran into a "hawk" or a "dove." The press gave the former name to those Americans who vehemently supported the nation's involvement in the fighting. The latter went to those who just as vehemently opposed the Vietnam War and the very idea of any war.

"The hawks were sore and embarrassed because America had lost and had gotten out of Vietnam," a California veteran recalls today. "I don't know how they talked themselves into blaming us, but they did. Somehow, they managed to forget that the U.S. pulled out of there not because the soldiers turned and ran but because the government decided it was time to leave."

This view of the hawks is substantiated by myriad stories the returnees were able to tell. The California veteran remembers going into a grocery store to buy a package of cigarettes a few weeks after his discharge. "I was still wearing my field jacket. The clerk took one look at it, made a face, and threw the pack down on the counter. It slid across and fell on the floor. He didn't say a thing, but I got the message—loud and clear."

Another veteran tells of meeting an elderly man who had served in World War I. The man looked at him and snarled a single word: "Loser." Still another recalls the husband and wife who visited his parents' home one evening. During dinner, the wife arched an eyebrow at him and said, "You people certainly didn't do much of a job over there, did you?"

And what of the doves? The California veteran remarks: "They were just as sore, especially the kids who had rebelled against the war. Only their anger was different. We weren't losers but killers. So far as they were concerned, we'd been taught to kill and then had gone out and murdered innocent civilians. It didn't do any good to tell them we hated the killing. Or that most of the people who were going to kill us weren't in uniform. We had no other choice. We had to defend ourselves against anyone who looked like a threat."

One experience with a dove involved a veteran who passed a young woman in hippie garb while he was out walking on one of his first days home. He was still wearing his uniform. The young woman stepped in front of him and spat in his face.

Many veterans heard their friends call them "suckers" for having allowed themselves to be sent to Vietnam and not to have fled the country instead. One vet recalls: "When I was drafted, I had a friend of mine tell me I was a fool for not taking off for Canada. I tried to explain that I didn't like the war any better than he did, but that I didn't want to mess up my life for years to come by breaking the law and evading the draft. I said I just wanted to get my military service over and done with so that I could get on with my life. All he did was look at me and call me a coward and a warmonger."

One of the worst incidents with a dove occurred when a veteran, on arriving in Seattle from overseas, went to a public telephone to make arrangements for the trip to his hometown. Just a few days before leaving Vietnam, he had been in hand-to-hand combat with Vietcong guerrillas. During the struggle, he had saved himself from death by sinking his teeth into a Vietcong fighter's neck. Now, as he talked on the telephone, he looked up to see a bearded young man getting ready to throw a tomato at him. The veteran charged his attacker and, with the memory of the hand-to-hand battle still sharply etched in his mind, bit deeply into the man's neck. Police arrived on the scene and pulled him away.

There were even some veterans who had trouble with their families. For example, one Arizona veteran remembers his older sister's vehement opposition to the war: "She was always telling me to go to Canada or Sweden or somewhere and live in peace. But I went to Nam instead. Then, when I got back home, she was living in an apartment across town, and she refused to come and see me on my first night back. She wouldn't have anything to do with me

/ 33 /

for months. At Christmas, she did come home, but she just sat at the dinner table and didn't say a thing. Wouldn't even look at me. It was years before she began to cool off."

It must be stressed again that many, if not most, veterans received warm welcomes from their friends and families. Nor were most spat upon, insulted, or shunned by the public. They knew that countless Americans, even those who most lamented the country's involvement in Vietnam, looked on them with sympathy and saw them as victims of the war. But they also knew that too many people saw them not as men who had served their country as best they could in a tragic situation but as warmongers, killers, fools, or poor fighters—in all, lowly creatures who were personally at fault for the whole hated mess. It was a knowledge that hurt deeply.

THREE PROBLEMS

The cold and often angry welcome home was bad enough in itself, but it was joined by a collection of problems suffered by many of the men. These were problems that, widely reported by the press, worsened their already poor image in the public eye. Knowing of their dismal image, some veterans felt an even deeper sense of alienation from their country.

First, it was known that there had been widespread drug and alcohol abuse among the troops in Vietnam and that the two difficulties were still troubling many of the men. Second, thousands of the veterans were said to be suffering from psychological ills, among them depression and a condition known as Post-Traumatic Stress Disorder (PTSD). Finally, the headlines of the 1970s left no doubt that many of the men were getting into trouble with the law.

In the next chapter, we'll talk about these problems in detail. They make up the second legacy to be discussed in this book. For now, let us just make two points. First, they were problems that plagued a minority of the 8.7 million Americans who served in the war. Second, despite the fact that they involved but a minority of the men, they tended to give *all* veterans a bad reputation. Although there were many Americans who felt that the problems were the understandable results of the horrors of battle and that the victims should be helped along the road to recovery, there were just as many others who wondered if the men were, as a class, weaklings; many who wondered if they could ever be trusted again as friends or fellow workers; many who feared and shunned them.

As the California veteran puts it today, it was "a case of guilt by association. Because some of the guys had problems, a lot of people thought we all had problems."

To many an American mind, there were valid reasons for the distrust and fear.[3] Throughout the 1970s, news reports spoke of veterans in trouble. In 1974, for example, an armed veteran made headlines when he roamed through a park in Los Angeles and took two park rangers prisoner. On being captured by police, he said that he had been out "on patrol" and that, since he had lived by the gun, he now wanted to die by the gun. Four years later, a study estimated that 29,000 veterans of the Vietnam era were in state or federal prisons.

Reports such as these could not help but make life difficult for veterans everywhere. The California veteran recalls several friends who had trouble finding work because they had been in uniform. "Employers didn't want anything to do with somebody who might be a drunk or a nut case. One of the guys finally kept his service a secret when he tried out for jobs."

Matters were not helped by the television and motion picture dramas of the day. The film and television industries have always used as dramatic themes the attitudes seen in the public at given times. Both did so in the late 1960s and then the 1970s. Repeatedly, they pictured the Vietnam veteran as so many people saw him—as anything from a crazed killer to a mindless drug addict.

From Hollywood, for example, came such films as *Apocalypse Now* (1979). It dealt with a soldier who is assigned to go on a mission that sees him surrounded by madmen, among them a savage officer who takes delight in bombing a Vietnamese village. And from television came dramas whose villains were troubled and dangerous veterans. For example, one episode of the once highly popular private-detective series *Mannix* featured a veteran who was a drug addict and sadist.

/ 35 /

THE TRUE PICTURE

The picture of the veteran as anything from a loser to an emotional cripple was, for most of the men, a badly mistaken one. The truth of the matter is that the vast majority of the returnees made a successful transition to civilian life and then lived successful lives.[4]

About two-thirds of the returnees enrolled in the nation's universities and colleges under the GI Bill of Rights. Among them were thousands who otherwise could not have afforded a higher education. The GI Bill, which had been enacted in the wake of World War II, paid part of the educational costs for veterans and provided them with funds to help meet daily living expenses. The percentage of Vietnam vets who returned to the nation's classrooms far exceeded that of the World War II returnees. Only about half of the World War II service people took advantage of the GI Bill.

Further, the Vietnam vets, as did most of the men who had fought in the century's earlier wars, achieved success in all fields of endeavor. Some started businesses of their own. Others joined the nation's industries, with some then rising to high executive positions. Still others, such as writer Donald McQuinn, the author of the acclaimed Vietnam novel *Targets,* earned respected places in the creative fields.

A recent government study revealed just how well the veterans have done through the years. Of the 15,000 veterans interviewed for the study, 90 percent said they were employed, while about 90 percent also reported being happy with their personal relationships. The study, which is called the Vietnam Experience Study, will be discussed in Chapter Four.

Among the veterans who won personal and professional success were those who returned with serious physical handicaps. One who lost the use of both legs in a vehicular accident while in service is now a successful Pacific Coast photographer. A badly wounded Rocky Bleier overcame his disability and became an outstanding running back with professional football's Chicago Bears. Robert Muller, whose wounds left him a paraplegic, founded and heads the Vietnam Veterans of America, a nationwide organization that works on behalf of all men and women who

Vietnam veteran Rocky Bleier, although badly wounded in the war, went on to achieve renown as a professional football player. He is shown here (No. 20) in 1978 playing for the Pittsburgh Steelers against the Cleveland Browns.

served in the war and seeks national and state legislation of value to them.

These nationally known figures were joined by others, many of whom made their mark in the nation's political life. More than fourteen Vietnam veterans have served in the U.S. Congress, among them Senators Albert Gore (Tennessee), Jeremiah Denton (Alabama), John Kerry (Massachusetts), and John McCain (Arizona), and Representatives Thomas Daschle (South Dakota) and James Kolbe (Arizona). Veterans Charles Robb of Virginia and Robert Kerrey of Nebraska have served as governors of their states.

A CHANGING NATIONAL ATTITUDE

The cold welcome home, the view of the veteran as anything from a loser to a piece of emotional wreckage, the terrible anger, guilt, and division that the war had triggered in the American public: all of these factors led to one result. For years after the war ended, the Vietnam veterans received from their fellow countrymen no recognition, no genuine sign of gratitude, no commemoration, for the service they had performed and the sacrifices they had made. Although they numbered in the millions, they seemed to be the forgotten of the nation. This forgetfulness added still more fuel to the alienation felt by so many.

Fortunately, the passing years, especially those of the 1980s, have brought a change of national attitude toward the veterans—and, with that change, has come a growing recognition of their service and sacrifice. The war is still remembered with a pain capable of touching the deepest of emotions, but the passage of time has begun to heal the raw wounds of old. The change in attitude that has evolved with the healing can be seen in a number of ways.

For one, a poll taken in 1979 by the Louis Harris organization revealed a major shift in public attitude. Of the people questioned in the poll, the number who had come to view the veterans as victims of the war was twice that of the people who still looked on them as "losers" or "warmongers." Nine years earlier, a public survey revealed that 50 percent of the people interviewed held the veterans in low esteem.[5]

Next, the television and motion picture industries, again reflecting widely held public views, have altered their depictions of the Vietnam veteran. No longer is he presented as a drug addict, an alcoholic, a psychotic, a criminal. Now, in such motion pictures as *Platoon, Uncommon Valor,* and the *Missing in Action* series, and in such television shows as *Magnum P.I.* and *Tour of Duty,* he comes across as a heroic figure, someone who did his best in an ugly war.[6]

Finally, an incident in 1981 must be mentioned. In January of that year, the fifty-two Americans who had been held hostage in Iran for months were at last all safely home. Their return was marked by a nationwide welcome. The veterans watched the happy tumult and, while thinking the welcome deserved, were nevertheless dismayed and angered. It seemed unfair that the nation should lavish so much attention on fifty-two people after ignoring the 8.7 million who had served in the war. Many veterans did not keep their anger to themselves. They voiced their feelings in marches, demonstrations, and press conferences. That many Americans felt as they did—felt that their service to the country had been too long ignored—was immediately seen in at least two ways. Contributions to the work of Robert Muller's Vietnam Veterans of America increased, as did donations to the building of a monument that would pay homage to all those who had died in the war—the Vietnam Veterans Memorial.[7]

The Vietnam Veterans Memorial

The story of the memorial, which stands as the single greatest tribute yet given for service in Vietnam, began in 1979 when veteran Jan Scruggs instituted the Vietnam Veterans Memorial Fund. Its aim was to raise $2.5 million for the construction of the monument in Washington, D.C.[8]

Scruggs began the fund with a $2,500 donation of his own. Then, working tirelessly, he succeeded in getting Congress to pass a bill setting aside two and a half acres in the nation's capital for the monument. He went on to win support for the memorial from such national figures as billionaire oil man Ross Perot and comedian Bob Hope. Hope, who had been entertaining U.S. troops ever since World War II, signed a fund-raising letter that was sent to more than a million Americans. Major financial and moral support came from Perot.

Next, Scruggs launched a competition meant to produce a design for the memorial. Some 1,420 designs were submitted to the contest, which was judged by an architectural committee. Chosen as the winner was a design by Maya Lin, a young woman studying architecture at Yale University. The Lin design called for two massive slabs of black granite, each 200 feet long. They were to be joined at a center point, with each then gently tapering away to the ground. On the walls would be inscribed the names of all those who had lost their lives in the war—close to 58,000 names in all.

When the Vietnam Veterans Memorial was dedicated on Veterans Day weekend in November 1982, more than a quarter million people traveled to Washington, D.C., to attend the ceremonies. Included in their number were thousands of veterans and their families, the families and friends of the men whose names were inscribed on the memorial, and countless Americans who knew that the time had come to pay homage to those who had sacrificed their lives in Vietnam.

Today, the memorial is visited daily by an unending stream of people—more than two million a year—who stop to whisper words of love and respect to lost ones, who leave notes and flowers in memory of the dead, and who have come to understand that the memorial stands not only as a tribute to the sacrifice made by the dead but also as a recognition of the service done by all those who served and survived.

Another memorial must be mentioned. For years, the war service performed by women—as service personnel, nurses, and civilians—was as overlooked as that of the men. In 1988, a first step toward rectifying this situation was taken by a U.S. Senate committee. The committee approved for Senate consideration a measure calling for the construction of a bronze statue of an Army nurse. The measure, which was introduced for consideration by

The grandeur of the Vietnam Veterans
Memorial in Washington, D.C., lies in
its simplicity: two massive slabs of
black granite, upon which are inscribed
the names of all those killed in the war
—close to 58,000 names in all.

Senators Alan Cranston (California) and David Durenberger (Minnesota), won congressional approval in October of that year. Congress indicated that it would like to see the statue placed on the site of the Veterans Memorial.[9]

The changing public attitude seen in recent times is bringing to an end one of the saddest legacies left to everyone who served in the Vietnam War. In time, it may be a legacy that will disappear altogether, taking with it the sense of alienation that it created.

There are two other equally sad legacies that have been left to the veterans. Both have to do with health problems suffered by thousands. We turn now to these terrible gifts.

THE SECOND

THE INVISIBLE WOUNDS

LEGACY

CHAPTER
THREE
INVISIBLE WOUNDS

Nearly 300,000 Americans who went to Vietnam were wounded or injured in the fighting, with some so badly hurt that they were left with severe physical disabilities for the rest of their lives. Additionally, many men suffered harms that have come to be called "invisible wounds." These wounds left no surface scars or lost limbs for the world to see. Damaged instead were the minds and emotions. This hidden damage showed itself in the three problems mentioned in Chapter Two that created so much public distrust and fear of all returning veterans.

The three problems, you'll recall, are drug and alcohol abuse, psychological ills, and troubles with the law. In percentages, the threesome plagued but a small proportion of the 8.7 million Americans who served in the war. In numbers, however, they were legacies that affected veterans in the thousands. They continue to trouble some to this day.

DRUG AND ALCOHOL ABUSE

Because of numerous press reports and tales brought back by returning veterans, Americans in the late 1960s and early 1970s knew full well that there was widespread drug and alcohol abuse among the troops in Vietnam and that both problems continued to trouble many men upon their release from service. Then, in the mid-1970s, the Department of Defense (DOD) released statistics showing how widespread the problems were.[1]

The statistics revealed that in the years 1968 to 1972 approximately 60 percent of the troops in Vietnam had smoked marijuana. About 30 percent had used hard drugs such as heroin. According to the DOD, one-fifth of all enlisted men serving in Vietnam during 1970 were addicted to some drug during their tour of duty.

Another set of statistics indicated the extent to which the problem remained after the men had been discharged. In 1971, a survey by the Louis Harris poll-taking organization showed that 26 percent of veterans continued taking drugs on leaving the service. (Happily, as we'll soon see, a government study made years later— in 1988—revealed a sharp decline in the problem.)

As for alcohol abuse, it was said to be widespread among the men who wanted nothing to do with drugs. The DOD held that between 5 percent and 10 percent of the veterans were in need of help with alcohol-related problems. A 1978 study ordered by President Jimmy Carter reported that alcoholics or problem drinkers made up about 13 percent of the men in Veterans Administration hospitals in 1970; the figure rose to 31 percent in 1977.

PSYCHOLOGICAL ILLS

For many Americans, the drug and alcohol problems were proof that the Vietnam veterans were a psychologically disturbed lot. That many of the men were indeed psychologically disturbed was borne out by studies conducted in the 1970s and 1980s. The veterans showed themselves to be suffering from such problems as depression, anxiety, and a disorder known as Post-Traumatic Stress Syndrome or Post-Traumatic Stress Disorder. Of the two terms, the latter is the more widely heard today and will be the one that we will use in this book.[2]

In the years following the war, many veterans turned to the Veterans Administration (VA) for help with their emotionally based problems, including drug and alcohol abuse. (Founded in 1930, the VA is the federal agency in charge of administering all laws pertaining to benefits for ex-service personnel and their dependents or beneficiaries.) So many sought help, in fact, that by the mid-1970s, the VA was spending about $2 billion a year on medical care, with a sizable portion of the funds going to the expansion of mental health and alcohol treatment facilities at its general and psychiatric hospitals across the nation.

The widespread need for psychiatric care in the 1970s, including drug and alcohol treatment, stretched the capacities of the Veterans Administration to the breaking point. Along with developing new treatment units and facilities, the VA had to develop new and highly efficient means for handling the influx of men in need of help. Prior to the Vietnam era, the VA had maintained no facilities for drug and alcohol patients.

Many of the men who sought assistance from the VA, their own physicians, or local private or public agencies were able to function and carry on their lives while being helped. Others required long-term hospitalization and treatment. Others were unable to carry the burden of their emotional ills and exploded in acts of violence. In one such case, an armed veteran entered a Massachusetts cemetery and opened fire on the people there. He continued firing until captured by the police. Fortunately, no one was injured.

Still other troubled veterans found life too hard to bear and attempted to take their own lives. The press reported in 1974 that close to one-quarter of the patients in VA hospitals had tried to kill themselves. There were 800,000 VA patients at the time.

Of the various psychological ills, Post-Traumatic Stress Disorder (PTSD) captured the greatest public attention over the years. It was the name given in the 1970s to a psychiatric illness that, in one form or another, had been seen in the wake of earlier wars. After World War I, the men who were suffering emotional or mental upset were described as being "shell-shocked." World War II and

Korean victims were said to be suffering from "battle fatigue." The condition became known as PTSD after Vietnam and has been the source of public and medical controversy ever since.

Just what is PTSD? The American Psychiatric Association defines it as a number of symptoms that take shape in the wake of a psychologically upsetting event. Such an event, like a war, is outside the range of normal human experience. The symptoms, which can appear in various combinations, include nightmares, startled reactions to events in the present, flashbacks to moments of great fear and stress (meaning the victim has the illusion that he is reliving the past event), and what is called "psychic numbing," a withdrawal from the surrounding world. It is a condition that may be slight or severe. It can strike at any time after the stressful event, even years afterward.

The first talk of Post-Traumatic Stress Disorder was heard in the late 1960s when psychiatrists noticed these symptoms in many veterans and began to wonder if the symptoms were all connected and were thus indications of a new psychological illness. Or were they separate problems—varied signs of such well-established disorders as depression or anxiety—that happened to strike certain men all at the same time? In all, was there or was there not such a thing as PTSD? For years, this question has been a matter of dispute among psychiatrists. Despite the American Psychiatric Association's definition, which was developed in the early 1980s, some psychiatrists doubt that PTSD actually exists (they are, however, thought to be in the minority today). Others feel certain that it does exist, but feel that more work is needed to clarify exactly what it is and how it affects its victims.

Other questions surround PTSD. One centers on how long the disorder may trouble a veteran. Some psychiatrists contend that PTSD is often of short duration, lasting less than six months. Others argue that it can last a lifetime and can be worsened by the stresses the veteran encounters at any time in life. The psychiatrists who hold the latter view believe that PTSD is incurable and that patients must be helped to live the rest of their lives with it.

Another question: How can the prevalence of PTSD among veterans be measured? Psychiatrists use definite measurements to

*Many Vietnam veterans suffered emotional trauma,
which came to be known as PTSD (post-traumatic
stress disorder). (Left) A bone-weary soldier stares
sightlessly into space after surviving a multi-battalion
operation along the Cambodian border in January 1966.
(Right) A Vietnam vet sits beneath a recruitment poster in
an outpatient clinic for the "psychologically disabled."*

detect the presence of other psychological disorders and know them to be accurate. These same measurements have been employed to measure the presence of PTSD but, for a variety of technical reasons, there is doubt that they do a proper job. If the tests are not trustworthy, there is no way of knowing whether PTSD or some other malady is actually behind the problems seen in the veterans.

These questions and others have affected the Vietnam veteran in very specific ways. First, some Americans have long doubted that there is such a thing as PTSD, and the psychiatric debate has fed that doubt. One World War II veteran says bluntly that the Vietnam men are "crybabies and complainers." He may be voicing the attitude of many who fought in World War II when he says that they, too, suffered the hardships and terrors of battle, but did so without going "psychologically to pieces" in great numbers. He contends that the terrors of battle are the same for all men, no matter the war, and so the Vietnam veterans are proving themselves weaklings when they complain of PTSD in great numbers.

Second, the questions and lingering doubts over PTSD have had a direct impact on whether a veteran can receive compensation and treatment when claiming to be a victim of the disorder.

The problem here can be seen by looking at the way applications for treatment and compensation are handled by the VA. To receive assistance for a service-connected psychological disorder, such as depression, a veteran must file a claim with the VA within one year of discharge from the service. However, for PTSD, since it is defined as being able to occur years after discharge, a veteran is permitted to file an application even if the disorder waits for decades before appearing. But the application will be approved only if the veteran can prove to a VA doctor's satisfaction that he is actually suffering the disorder.

And so the questions and conflicting viewpoints surrounding PTSD present the veteran with a dilemma upon submitting his application. How can he prove his claim when there is an argument among psychiatrists as to whether PTSD actually exists? How can he prove the degree of his illness—and thus the degree and length of VA care he needs—when there is doubt over the measurements used to assess PTSD's presence and when there is divided opinion over the length of time it afflicts a veteran? And, because PTSD seems able to strike long after the event that caused it, how can he prove that his ills today are linked to something that happened years ago?

A VA study in 1981 estimated that some 700,000 veterans were affected by PTSD. The study, known as the *Legacies of Vietnam,* investigated the mental health of 1,440 veterans and projected the 700,000 figure on the basis of its findings. Despite the controversy, the Veterans Administration has made disability payments to more than 18,000 veterans who have claimed to be suffering the disorder.

In 1988 the results of yet another VA study—the National Vietnam Veterans Readjustment (NVVR) study—were made known to the U.S. Senate Committee on Veterans' Affairs. The NVVR study began in 1984 and reviewed the health histories of more than 2,000 veterans, men and women alike. By projecting its findings, it estimated that approximately 470,000 of the more than three million men who served in Vietnam are currently suffering PTSD. Suffering with them are approximately 650 of the 7,000 women who went to Vietnam.

Regardless of the above mentioned VA payments and the *Legacies* and NVVR studies, the questions about PTSD still remain. They need to be pursued and resolved in fairness to all veterans and the public at large—in fairness to the veterans who are being labeled "crybabies" when in fact they may be seriously ill men, and in fairness to the public because it has the right to know whether its tax money is being spent to help veterans who are actually ill.

CRIMINAL ACTIVITIES

In addition to detailing all the drug, alcohol, and psychological problems, the press in the 1960s and 1970s reported on the many veterans who were in trouble with the law.3 As you'll recall from Chapter Two, a study made on orders from President Jimmy Carter

/ 51 / SENIOR HIGH SCHOOL LIBRARY
SUNNYSIDE, WASHINGTON

was widely headlined when it estimated that 29,000 veterans of the Vietnam era were in state and federal penitentiaries. (The term *Vietnam-era* is used here because the study did not specify how many of the veterans had served in Vietnam and how many had served elsewhere. Since the two groups were lumped together, no conclusions could be made as to how greatly actual service in Vietnam had contributed to later criminal activities.)

The study also disclosed that another 250,000 veterans were on probation, 35,000 had been released from prison and were on parole, and just over 87,000 were awaiting trial. Altogether, including the 29,000 in prison, the number of veterans in trouble with the law totaled 401,000. The number was distressingly high, but it still added up to only about 5 percent of the 8.7 million veterans who had served in the war, either in Vietnam or elsewhere. The vast majority of veterans were living productive and law-abiding lives.

The crimes for which the veterans stood charged were of all varieties. They ranged from acts of violence to drug dealing and abuse to burglary, car theft, and armed robbery. Although there were violent crimes that made the headlines, the *Legacies of Vietnam* study in 1981 reported that most of the offenses had been of a nonviolent nature.

WHY THE PROBLEMS?

The answer to this question is a complex one. It is made up of many factors. Those factors range from the feelings of the veterans about the war to the conditions they faced in Vietnam.[4]

According to psychiatrists, psychologists, and social workers who have dealt with troubled veterans, the conditions in Vietnam had much to do with the drug and alcohol abuse there. A study made in the early 1980s of 100 veterans reported that some men used drugs and alcohol to escape their fears and the horrors they had seen in combat. Others turned to drugs and alcohol to ease their homesickness. (Although homesickness has played a part in every war, it may have played an especially great role in Vietnam because of the very young age of the men who fought there. The average age of the Vietnam soldier was nineteen; the average age of service for World War II was twenty-six.) Still others used drugs to continue functioning in battle. They took amphetamines to ward off fatigue and then, when the time came to rest, turned to sedative-type drugs to help them relax.

Guilt accounted for much of the drug and alcohol abuse seen during the war and for many of the psychological problems that came to light in later years. One soldier began drinking heavily after he accidentally killed a small child. The California veteran whose views were quoted in Chapter Two believes that he is speaking for many veterans when he talks of his own sense of guilt and how it took shape:

"Every war is a filthy business. But Vietnam, I think, must have been the dirtiest of them all. In most wars, you've got a recognizable enemy to shoot at. He's in uniform. But, in Nam, you had to shoot at practically everybody to make sure that you didn't get killed. The Vietcong and all the people who supported them weren't in uniform. Anybody could have been the enemy, ready to knife you or toss a grenade at you. And so you did what you had to do. It hurt when you killed someone because you didn't know whether you were getting a Vietcong or some poor peasant. It hurt really bad if it was a woman or a kid.

"It goes without saying that civilians were hurt and killed and lost their homes in the world wars and Korea. But things seemed to be different then. The soldiers could think of them as victims of the whole situation. Since the guys weren't shooting at them, they didn't feel personally responsible for what was happening to the civilians. But a lot of men did feel personally responsible in Nam. A lot of guys just couldn't handle it."

Anger also played a part in the three problems. During the war and the subsequent years, many men expressed a rage at having been forced into a conflict that, along with a vast segment of the American public, they hated. Many were angry at having been made to kill after being taught in childhood that killing was wrong. And, of course, there was the anger over the cold welcome home and over the widespread public view that the Vietnam veteran was a "loser" or a "warmonger."

The rage triggered outbreaks of violence, such as the shooting in the Massachusetts cemetery, and caused deep-seated feelings of depression. In 1974, a social worker with the Veterans Administration said that Vietnam veterans were angry and wanted society to bleed as much as they had.

There seems little doubt that the horrors of battle played a major role in the three problems. In the area of criminal activities, for example, the *Legacies of Vietnam* study reported that most of the veterans who had been placed under arrest since the war's end were men who had endured heavy combat. Their arrest rate was about three times that of veterans who had gone through light combat or no combat at all.

In 1988, in commenting on Post-Traumatic Stress Disorder, sociologist Robert Laufer of the City College of New York said that studies have consistently shown that the presence of PTSD depends on how much death and dying a man saw in Vietnam. Laufer explained that three factors are crucial in predicting a soldier's later problems with PTSD: moderate to heavy combat, the loss of fellow soldiers, and the witnessing of or the participating in violence or atrocities.

Actually, any attempt to answer the question "Why the problems?" produces more questions than answers. Many Americans suspect that the World War II veteran may be right when, as quoted earlier, he says that the experience of combat was just as awful in preceding wars and that the troubled Vietnam veterans are "crybabies and complainers." On the other hand, many people believe there may have been something special about the Vietnam War—perhaps the widespread hatred and shame it engendered—that made it totally different from the earlier wars and, as a result, left so many men emotionally crushed.

Still others wonder if there was something in the spirits and backgrounds of the men that made their emotions especially vulnerable to harm. Was there something in their personalities or upbringing that made them "complainers" and "crybabies"? Or was there something in their upbringing, something in twentieth-century American society, that made them more sensitive than the men who fought before them?

Vietnam veterans make up part of the homeless population. Here, after the first snowfall of the season in November 1987, a homeless man lies under a sheet of clear plastic that serves as a blanket. In the background is the White House.

Finally, many wonder whether the war itself actually caused some of the problems. The veterans of every war have always had among their number men who committed crimes, men who were alcoholics, men who were left emotionally crippled, and men who could not find a place for themselves in their country's life. And so a plaguing question for all the years since the Vietnam War's end has been: Was the war itself completely responsible for the troubles suffered by the veterans? Or were some of the men, because of their frailties, responsible? Would they have lived troubled lives even if there had been no Vietnam?

These are questions that may never be answered.

CHAPTER
FOUR

HOW WELL HAVE
THE VETERANS FARED?

We've stressed several times now that the invisible wounds and their three problems struck only a small percentage of the Americans who served in the war. We know that the great bulk of the Vietnam veterans have lived successful lives. But just how well have they fared in matters of health, both mental and physical? An answer is needed if we're to have a balanced picture of what the war did—or did not do—to the people who fought it.

In recent years, a number of studies, among them the *Legacies of Vietnam,* have attempted to ascertain the various physical and psychological problems that stemmed from service in the war. Of all the investigations, the largest is known as The Vietnam Experience Study.[1] Financed with government funds, it was conducted over a period of four years by the Centers for Disease Control (CDC) at Atlanta, Georgia.

THE VIETNAM EXPERIENCE STUDY

Involved in the study were some 15,000 veterans and hundreds of medical doctors, psychologists, and psychiatrists. The veterans were men who had served in the military between 1965 and 1971. They were divided into two groups. The first group consisted of 7,924 men who had served in Vietnam. Making up the second group—which was known as the control group—were 7,364 men who had served elsewhere, in more peaceful surroundings. The physical and psychological findings that emerged from the groups were compared to answer two basic questions. First, were the men who had served in Vietnam suffering more problems than the men in the control group, the men who had not gone to Vietnam? Second, were the Vietnam men suffering more intensely from problems that were also seen in the non-Vietnam men?

Just as the men were split into two groups, so was the study divided into two parts. The first was made up of lengthy telephone interviews with all 15,000 veterans. The interviewers asked general questions about the health of the men and specific questions about physical and psychological problems. Then, about 35 percent of the men in each group were given extensive physical and psychological examinations.

The results of the study were announced in the summer of 1988. Here is what the CDC researchers found.

PSYCHOLOGICAL HEALTH

Clearly shown by the study was the fact that the men who served in Vietnam had suffered more from psychological problems than had their counterparts. They showed themselves to have been more prone to depression, anxiety, and alcoholism through the years since they were in uniform.

For example, the study showed that 15 percent of the men who served in Vietnam reported having experienced Post-Traumatic Stress Disorder. The veterans said they had suffered PTSD at some time during the years since they were in service. About 2 percent said that they were having trouble with the problem at the time of the study.

Further, about 14 percent of the Vietnam men admitted to a current problem with alcohol dependence or abuse; 9 percent of the control group admitted to the same problems. About 5 percent of the Vietnam men suffer from what is called "major clinical depression" as opposed to 2 percent among the control group. The same percentages apply for a generalized feeling of anxiety—5 percent among the Vietnam men as opposed to 2 percent among the control group.

Although the CDC researchers found these problems serious, they pointed out that the problems are affecting only a small minority of men. These problems, they wrote, "are not of a magnitude" that has kept the Vietnam men, as a group, from functioning successfully in their professional and personal lives.

According to the study, the great majority of the men in both groups are today leading successful lives. About 90 percent of the men in both groups reported being employed. About 90 percent in both groups also stated that they are happy with their personal relationships. Some 60 percent of all those who had married said they were still married to their first wives.

One aspect of the study—an aspect that also indicates that most veterans are today living successful lives—surprised the CDC researchers. They found drug abuse to be very low in both groups—about 0.5 percent in each. The finding could not help but come as a surprise after all the years of hearing about the widespread drug problem among the veterans.

PHYSICAL HEALTH

The men who had served in Vietnam showed a greater hearing loss than did their control group counterparts. The greatest loss was seen among the veterans who had served in battle. Obviously at fault here was the noise of battle.

Samples of semen were taken from the two groups. The samples showed that the men who had served in Vietnam were twice as likely as their counterparts to have a low sperm count and one and a half times as likely to have low levels of normal sperm cells.

This finding caused many people to wonder if the low count and low levels were the results of being exposed to the herbicide Agent Orange that had been sprayed over great areas of Vietnam. In the years since the war's end, thousands of veterans have claimed that their exposure to Agent Orange had damaged their health and was responsible for such tragedies as miscarriages among their wives and birth defects among their children. The herbicide and the possible damage it has done are the subjects of the next chapters.

The CDC researchers said that the low counts had not affected the ability of the men to father children. They added that their search of hospital records did not reveal a greater incidence of birth defects among the children of the men who had served in Vietnam than among the children of the control group men.

In answering the questions asked during the telephone calls to both groups, the men who had served in Vietnam showed themselves to be twice as likely to report health problems of some sort: 19.6 percent voiced health complaints in comparison to 11.1 percent of the control group. However, in the physical examinations that followed the calls, doctors could detect few medical differences between the representatives of the two groups. So that there would be no chance of bias, the doctors did not know which of the men had been in Vietnam and which had not.

The CDC researchers said that the Vietnam men may have reported more symptoms and past medical conditions because they had experienced more stress than the control group during the war.

A CURIOUS DISCOVERY

While the CDC researchers found the veterans who had served in Vietnam to be in better overall health than the public had been led to believe, they did come across an odd fact concerning those with psychological problems. The prevalence of those problems was tied to the dates the men had entered the military service.

What was found was this: The men who had been sent to Vietnam between 1965 and 1967 showed themselves to be twice as likely to have current psychological problems. The percentage of problems leveled off in 1968 and then decreased among the men who had served in Vietnam after 1968.

On looking at this finding, the CDC researchers said that, obviously, some sort of change had taken place in the men around 1968. They could not pinpoint that change, but they offered several possibilities.

For one, they pointed out that the anti-war sentiment in the United States, after growing over the years, reached its zenith in 1968. The year was marked by such violence as the street fighting that broke out between police and anti-war demonstrators during the Democratic National Convention at Chicago. The year also witnessed the Tet offensive, the massive Vietcong and North Vietnamese attack that, although finally beaten back with terrible enemy losses, brought countless Americans to the realization that their country could not hope to win the war in the long run. The enemy was all too willing to commit an endless number of men to the conflict for there to be substance to any such hope.

The CDC researchers suggested that the men who were sent to Vietnam between 1965 and 1967 were more supportive of the war and more idealistic about their country's participation in it. The growing anti-war sentiment and the terrible events of 1968 then shocked them so deeply that the door to future psychological disturbances swung open.

On the other hand, the men who went to Vietnam in the years after 1968 were accustomed to the anti-war sentiment, were probably opposed to the war themselves, and were less idealistic about their country's participation. Consequently, they were less vulnerable to psychological upsets.

In summary, the Vietnam veteran is in better health, physically and mentally, and is leading a more successful life than was hitherto thought. Although the veterans with drug, alcohol, psychiatric, and criminal problems may never escape their fate, and although they are deserving of the nation's sympathy and help, it is good to know that at least one legacy of the Vietnam War is not—and perhaps never was—as widespread and tragic as was once thought.

THE THIRD LEGACY

AGENT ORANGE

CHAPTER
FIVE
THE MYSTERY OF AGENT ORANGE

In 1962, the U.S. Air Force launched a series of unusual bombing strikes in South Vietnam and Laos. The strikes were leveled against the Vietcong and were unusual because they did not send bombs raining down on the enemy. Rather, sweeping low, C-123 cargo planes unleashed cloudy streams of a liquid that drenched the jungle foliage and spattered the bushes along roadsides and paths. The attacks bore the name Operation Ranch Hand. The liquid was the weed and plant killer called Agent Orange.

OPERATION RANCH HAND AND AGENT ORANGE

Operation Ranch Hand planned to do two jobs with Agent Orange.[1] First, it aimed to have the herbicide put an end to the successful guerrilla war being fought by the Vietcong in South Vietnam. Much of the enemy's success hinged on a wise use of the country's jungles. Vietcong fighters were constantly attacking from the dense growth and then fading back into it to hide from the U.S.

ground and air forces. They were also using the Laotian jungles to conceal a string of secret training bases. Operation Ranch Hand was to strip away all this protective cover by defoliating the jungle lands with Agent Orange. *Defoliating* means that foliage is made to lose its leaves.

Ranch Hand's second job stemmed from the fact that the Vietcong were "living off the land." They were taking and using the crops grown by South Vietnamese farmers. By dumping Agent Orange on the country's farmlands, the operation planned to deprive the guerrilla troops of a vital food supply.

Operation Ranch Hand lasted from 1962 to 1970. Actually, there had been sprayings of Vietcong cover with various herbicides, Agent Orange among them, since 1961. Between that year and the end of Ranch Hand, more than 17 million gallons of herbicides were dumped on Vietnam, with Agent Orange accounting for some 11 to 12 million of those gallons. Estimates hold that 5 to 15 percent of the country's area was doused with the chemical. The U.S. Navy sprayed the banks of South Vietnam's rivers in an effort to protect its patrol boats from ambush. In addition, Army servicemen attacked the underbrush in battle areas with hand-held sprayers. All the various sprayings caused Agent Orange to affect the lives of countless people—American and Vietnamese alike.

Thousands of American personnel in Vietnam were exposed to the chemical. Some handled it during its shipment overseas or while it was being loaded aboard the C-123s. Others served in areas that had been sprayed or were currently being defoliated. Also exposed were multitudes of Vietnamese civilians and fighters.

Ranch Hand was judged a success because it caused a sharp drop in the risk of surprise attacks from the jungle growth. Before the riverbanks were sprayed, for example, the men on the patrol boats had a 6 percent chance of being killed or wounded in any month; their casualty rate dropped to 1 percent per month following the sprayings. But the years since the war have seen a great number of sad developments that have caused both the American and Vietnamese people to wonder if Agent Orange, while hin-

/ 66 /

Dr. Matthew Meselson, a member of the Herbicide Assessment Commission of the American Association for the Advancement of Science (AAAS), shows photographs taken in 1969 of forest lands in Vietnam before and after military herbicide spraying. The commission reported that defoliation resulted in the destruction of enough food to feed 600,000 persons for one year.

dering the attacks of the Vietcong, did not launch an insidious attack of its own.

Because of these developments, both countries have been haunted by two terrible questions about the people who were exposed to Agent Orange: Did the chemical harm their health and leave them damaged for the rest of their lives? Did it reach out and endanger the health of their spouses and children?

A LEGACY OF ILLNESS?

When Agent Orange was first dropped, the U.S. military did not think it posed a threat to human health.[2] The next years, however, brought a number of alarming reports. They all indicated that the herbicide might indeed be dangerous. American authorities were told of a sharp rise in the number of Vietnamese children being born with birth defects. These reports, along with stories of American personnel in sprayed areas falling strangely ill, prompted the military to call off Operation Ranch Hand in 1970. Seven years later, in the wake of Agent Orange studies done with animals, the United States destroyed its supply of the herbicide.

The years since Operation Ranch Hand have seen an increasing number of Vietnam veterans report various health problems that they suspect are the result of being exposed to Agent Orange. Between 50,000 and 60,000 veterans have taken their illnesses and suspicions to VA hospitals. They have arrived with liver problems and various cancers. Many have spoken of their wives suffering miscarriages. And many have complained of their children being born with birth defects, among them, deformed limbs, cleft palates, and spina bifida. (Cleft palate is an opening or fissure in the roof of the mouth; spina bifida is a defect in the bony wall of the spinal canal.)

Additionally, Vietnam has reported a growing number of maladies that might have come from exposure to the herbicide. For example, when American reporter Robert Shaplen visited Ho Chi Minh City in the mid-1980s, he came face-to-face with what were claimed to be tragedies inflicted on the unborn by Agent Orange and other chemicals. In his book, *Bitter Victory,* he wrote that he

/ 68 /

toured a hospital where he was shown an exhibit made up chiefly of deformed fetuses; some were without brains, while others had enlarged heads.

Shaplen was then escorted through a ward for young girls. All the patients there were marked with hydratiform moles, which are clusters of abnormal formations. A hospital doctor told the journalist that cases in which the moles turned into cancerous tumors had been increasing over recent years. The physician produced statistics showing that the number of such cases and other health problems were at their highest in areas where the Vietcong had been most active and were therefore areas that had been hardest hit by Agent Orange attacks.

The U.S. and Vietnamese reports have triggered a great mystery. Although the people who were exposed to Agent Orange strongly suspect that it harmed them and their loved ones, they cannot be absolutely sure that the chemical was actually at fault. No one can. This is because several recent studies of Agent Orange victims have failed to show a definite link between the herbicide and human illness.

THE MYSTERY
OF AGENT ORANGE

Agent Orange got its name from the bright orange stripes on the 55-gallon steel drums in which it was shipped to Vietnam.[3] It is a member of the chemical family known as organo-halogen compounds.[4] These are substances in which bromine, chlorine, or fluorine is mixed with organic chemicals. They have found widespread use as herbicides, pesticides, solvents, and fire retardants. They also serve as raw materials in the manufacture of plastic products.

Agent Orange is produced by combining approximately equal amounts of two acids—2,4-D (dichlorophenoxyacetic acid) and 2,4,5-T (trichlorophenoxyacetic acid). On its own, the herbicide is not considered unusually dangerous to human health. But a compound that takes shape during its manufacture is another story.

This by-product appears in small and variable amounts during manufacture and is known as TCDD, with the initials coming from key letters in its chemical name—*tetra*chloro*di*benzo-p-*d*ioxin. Most often, scientists simply call it *dioxin*. First developed for chemical warfare during World War II, dioxin is recognized as a highly toxic substance. When in the presence of chemicals that are mildly carcinogenic, it is known to turn them highly carcinogenic (cancer-causing). And, when tested on laboratory animals, it has caused death in some and has triggered liver disorders, birth defects, and various cancers in others.

While its dangers to animals are well established, the effects of dioxin on human beings has always been a matter of question. As said earlier, several studies of humans exposed to Agent Orange have been conducted in recent years. Their findings have all been judged to be inconclusive. Although some indications of possible harm have been noted, the researchers in charge of the studies say that, to date, they have been unable to establish a definite, beyond-doubt link between Agent Orange's dioxin content and human illness.

There are two possible exceptions here. First, on the basis of two studies made in Sweden some years ago, Agent Orange is strongly suspected of being the cause of a skin disorder called chloracne.[5] Chloracne is a painful and disfiguring rash. The suspicion that Agent Orange causes the eruption took shape in 1976 when an explosion at a chemical plant in Italy released a giant dioxin cloud over a nearby village. The accident was followed by a widespread outbreak of chloracne among the villagers, plus the death of many animals.

Second, the herbicide's dioxin is strongly suspected of causing soft tissue sarcoma, a rare form of cancer that strikes such body areas as muscles and connective tissues. It is a cancer that has been widely noted in workers who have been exposed to large amounts of dioxin during the manufacture of Agent Orange.

Although a definite link between Agent Orange and human illness has not yet been established, there are thousands of American ex-servicemen who have no doubts about the herbicide's villainy. Their belief is rooted in the myriad stories of illness that they can tell. Here are just three.

The Ryan Experience

On arriving in Vietnam in 1966, Pfc Michael Ryan was sent into an area that had been sprayed with Agent Orange. Soon thereafter, he suffered an outbreak of mysterious lumps in the groin area and a rash all over his body. He also suddenly lost fifty pounds. Despite his problems, Ryan remained on active duty with the help of penicillin. Then, some years after his discharge from the Army, he became the father of a baby daughter. The infant was born with malformed organs and limbs, and a hole in her heart. She will spend her life in a wheelchair.[6]

The Zumwalt Experience

A particularly well-known story concerns Elmo Zumwalt III.[7] His experience was widely reported in the press because he was the son of Admiral Elmo Zumwalt, Jr., the commander in chief of the U.S. naval forces in Vietnam from 1968 to 1970. For a time, the young Zumwalt commanded a Navy patrol boat on a river whose banks had been defoliated by Agent Orange. Along with bathing in the river, he and his crew ate the local food and drank the local water because the boat was so far from a supply base. In subsequent years, Zumwalt suffered two types of cancer—lymphoma and Hodgkin's disease. The former produces tumors in the lymphoid tissues. The latter, along with attacking the lymphoid tissues, strikes at the spleen and the lymph nodes. Zumwalt died of his cancers in August 1988.

Additionally, Zumwalt's young son is suspected of having the birth disorder known as sensory integration dysfunction, a condition that makes it difficult for the child to concentrate and to perceive the differences in various sights and sounds. It has delayed the development of the boy's ability to do such things as walk and talk.

Zumwalt believed that his and his son's problems stemmed from exposure to Agent Orange. In a 1987 issue of *Health* magazine, he spoke of why he saw a connection between the herbicide and his lymphoma. He pointed out that lymphoma usually attacks people in their fifties. Why is it, then, he asked, that physicians at the National Cancer Institute and other medical facilities across the

Elmo Zumwalt III (left), *shown here in September 1986 with his father, Admiral Elmo Zumwalt, Jr., and his son, Russell, died in 1988 of cancer attributed to exposure to Agent Orange in Vietnam. Russell is suspected of having a birth disorder traceable to his father's exposure to the herbicide.*

country have been encountering so many cases of lymphoma in Vietnam veterans—men who are still in their twenties and thirties?

The Zumwalt case is not only well known but is also considered highly ironic. It was Zumwalt's father who, while commanding the naval forces in Vietnam, ordered that the country's riverbanks be sprayed with Agent Orange to protect the U.S. patrol boats from ambush. At that time, the admiral did not know of the herbicide's possible dangers to humans.

The Malloy Experience

But service personnel are not the only ones who have reported health problems after exposure to Agent Orange. Complaints have also come from civilians who went to Vietnam. When Kammy McCleery Malloy was a Red Cross worker in Vietnam, she showered with water that she now suspects was stored in empty Agent Orange drums.[8] She also entered areas that had been defoliated with the chemical. Now she has found that she can have no more children. She blames Agent Orange for the problem.

Some 2,000 Red Cross workers, as well as an undetermined number of civilians with other agencies—mostly women—served in Vietnam. Some have suffered skin disorders and such problems as infertility, miscarriages, and cervical cancer. A number of their children have been born with birth defects. Malloy herself underwent a hysterectomy (a surgical procedure that removes the uterus) after large fibroid tumors were discovered in the uterus during the birth of her first child. She also suffers from respiratory problems, rashes, and lesions in the scalp. She has had thirty skin tumors removed.

The mystery and the many suspicions surrounding Agent Orange eventually led to two courses of action in the 1980s. The actions were taken along the medical and legal fronts.

A number of medical studies were done on the possible harm caused by the herbicide. In addition, veterans who claimed to have suffered damage spent long years pursuing a lawsuit to win financial compensation for their ills.

The next chapter will report on the two courses of action.

/ 73 /

CHAPTER
SIX

MEDICAL AND
LEGAL ACTIONS

Three large-scale medical studies on Agent Orange marked the 1980s. All three were government-sponsored. Two were conducted in the United States and one in Australia.

THREE MEDICAL STUDIES

The first of the American studies focused on a group of Air Force men who had participated in Operation Ranch Hand. The second, conducted by the Centers for Disease Control in Atlanta, Georgia, concentrated on the birth defects suffered by the children of veterans who had been exposed to Agent Orange. The Australian effort looked at the health of 1,560 of the 47,000 soldiers the country had sent to Vietnam.

The results of the studies were announced in 1984. The Air Force study of the Ranch Hand men was the first to make its findings public.

The Ranch Hand Study

Investigated here were 1,045 officers and enlisted men.[1] They were subjected to a battery of questionnaires and a series of medical examinations as the study looked into such matters as their general physical and mental health, the incidence of cancer among them, the incidence of disorders of the major organ systems, and the incidence of birth defects in their children. The findings that emerged from all the testing were then compared to findings derived from a study of a control group—a group of Air Force men who had not participated in the Ranch Hand "bombings."

The results of the study were released by its research team in February 1984. The researchers announced that they had not found sufficient evidence to indict Agent Orange as the cause of any adverse health problems. They said that many of the tests had shown no statistical difference between the health problems suffered by the Ranch Hand group and the control group. In all, the Ranch Handers did not appear to be significantly more prone to illness than the non–Ranch Handers.

Much of this opinion was based on the fact that two illnesses closely linked with Agent Orange—chloracne and soft tissue sarcoma—were not elevated among the Ranch Handers. This means that the Ranch Handers did not show a significantly greater incidence of these disorders than did the control group.

The researchers, however, did not go so far as to say that the absence of these disorders meant that the two had no possible link with Agent Orange. Rather, they explained that the absence of chloracne could mean that the Ranch Handers had been exposed to lesser amounts of dioxin than the factory workers among whom the rash was so frequently seen. As for soft tissue sarcoma, they held that several factors could account for its absence. Those factors included the small size of the Ranch Hand group, the rarity of the cancer itself, and the extended length of time the disease takes to develop. Sarcoma may not have shown itself in such a small group or may not yet have had the time it needed to develop.

Although free of two highly suspect problems, the Ranch Handers revealed a higher than normal incidence of some other disorders. For one, they suffered a somewhat higher percentage of liver disorders—1.56 percent as compared to 0.78 percent for the non–Ranch Handers.

Additionally, the children born of the Ranch Handers seemed to suffer more than those fathered by men in the control group.

There was a greater percentage of deaths among the Ranch Hand newborns—1.7 percent as opposed to 0.4 percent. And there was a greater percentage of minor birth defects, such as birthmarks—9.1 percent as compared to 6.5 percent.

The researchers, however, did not think that the various percentage differences in the Ranch Handers and their children were great enough to suggest a definite link to Agent Orange. They also pointed out that factors other than exposure to the herbicide showed themselves as possible causes of some of the problems. These factors included alcohol consumption and heavy smoking.

In all, the results of the study were characterized as being inconclusive. Although there were indications that Agent Orange might have caused trouble in some areas, the researchers said that they could not find among the Ranch Handers a set of symptoms or a pattern of symptoms to suggest a solid connection between present-day health problems and exposure to Agent Orange in the past.

The Children of Atlanta

The study by the Centers for Disease Control (CDC) involved about 8,000 children who had been born in the Atlanta metropolitan area between 1968 and 1980.[2] Approximately 4,800 of the youngsters had birth defects, some minor, others major. Of the 8,000 children studied, 696 had been fathered by Vietnam veterans who claimed to have been exposed to Agent Orange. Four hundred and twenty-eight of the veterans' children were marred to one degree or another by birth defects.

When the results of the study were announced in the summer of 1984, the CDC researchers said they had found that, in general, the Vietnam veterans ran no greater risk of fathering children with birth defects than did the general Atlanta public. They reported seeing no greater incidence of birth defects among the veterans' children than among the youngsters of other Atlanta parents. Their conclusion: There seemed to be no definite link between birth defects and Agent Orange.

The researchers, however, did say that some of the children appeared to run a higher risk of being born with any of several specific problems. The youngsters were those who had been born of fathers who had served in Vietnamese areas that had received the heaviest Orange sprayings. Their problems included spina bifida, cleft palate, and certain tumors.

Nevertheless, the CDC researchers claimed that they were unable to make a definite connection between these disorders and Agent Orange. As did the Ranch Hand investigators, they said that such factors as alcohol consumption and heavy smoking among the parents might well have accounted for—or contributed to—the defects.

The results of the CDC study matched those of the Ranch Hand investigation in that they were deemed inconclusive. The CDC researchers had seen some harms but could not say that they were definitely the result of exposure to Agent Orange.

The Australian Study

When published in late 1984, the report of the Australian findings ran to 3,000 pages and was more strongly worded than those of the U.S. studies.[3] It labeled as "quite unfounded" the fears that Agent Orange induced health problems. It contended that the children of the 1,580 veterans in the study ran no greater risk of birth defects than did other youngsters.

The study went on to say that such common complaints as headaches, ulcers, and depression heard among the veterans could be attributed to stress rather than a past exposure to Agent Orange. It then held that some of the problems seen in the study were likely caused by the same factors noted in the Ranch Hand and CDC studies—alcohol consumption and heavy smoking.

Overall, the study found the Australian veterans to be healthier than the average citizen.

Under Critical Fire

The three studies came under sharp critical fire when their results were announced.[4] Many Australian veterans condemned their nation's study on the grounds that its findings were intended to keep the government from paying them the compensation they might seek for their ills and the birth defects seen in their children.

In the United States, a basic criticism of the Ranch Hand study held that it had made a mistake in limiting its investigation to Air Force personnel. The study had claimed that Air Force men had been the personnel most exposed to Agent Orange. The critics argued that ground troops had also been heavily exposed and so should have been included in the study. Because they had been omitted, the investigation had to be looked on as incomplete. The same complaint came from the American women who had served in Vietnam as staff workers, nurses, and Red Cross workers.

Both the Ranch Hand and CDC researchers were attacked for saying that many of the problems they had noted could not be solidly linked to Agent Orange. Samuel Epstein, a specialist in occupational and environmental medicine with the University of Illinois Medical Center at Chicago, said that the CDC findings of spina bifida and certain tumors in the veterans' children made it difficult to think that there was not a strong relationship between them and the herbicide.

Joining in this criticism was Ellen Silbergeld, a scientist with the Environmental Defense Fund. She said that many of the ills noted in the two studies—in the children and the veterans alike—mirrored those observed in studies of the effects of toxic substances on animals.

Much criticism of the two studies stemmed from the federal government's view of the dangers of Agent Orange. The government had long contended that, with the exception of chloracne, the herbicide had done no harm. The critics accused the government of taking this stand to avoid the heavy costs of paying all the veterans who would seek compensation for their ills. They then charged that the two studies had tended to come up with findings that supported the government's view because both had been federally funded. Many of the critics did not accuse the researchers of being biased, but contended that they might not have pursued all avenues of their research as vigorously as possible.

Veterans groups—among them the Vietnam Veterans Agent Orange Victims, a nationwide organization dedicated to furthering the cause of the herbicide victims—and a number of national legislators spoke out against the two studies. They all called for further investigations into the health threats posed by Agent Orange. The Ranch Hand researchers replied that they had always planned to check on their subjects in the following year and at five-year intervals thereafter. The periodic checks are scheduled to continue until the year 2002.

The Latest Word

At the time this book is being written, the question of Agent Orange's connection with human illness remains unanswered. But some answers may be on the way. A number of institutions, among them the National Cancer Institute, are doing studies of farmers who handled Agent Orange and factory workers who suffered accidents with the herbicide. The principal objective here is to see if the health experiences of these people are akin to the illnesses of the exposed veterans. To date, the researchers have studied farmers and workers in the U.S., Italy, Japan, Sweden, and West Germany. They claim to have found indications linking the herbicide to various cancers—including soft tissue sarcoma—and to a liver disorder known as porpheria.[5]

In recent years, a number of states have launched Agent Orange studies, doing so out of concern for the health not only of their ex-servicemen but also of their chemical workers.[6] Among them are Connecticut, Delaware, Florida, Illinois, Massachusetts, Michigan, New Jersey, Oklahoma, Pennsylvania, Rhode Island, Virginia, and West Virginia.

The states have accomplished much in their Agent Orange work. For example, the twelve listed above have banded together to form the National Association of State Agent Orange Programs. They hope to do improved work through the association by pooling their research facilities. Their plans call for them to take the association's findings and the cause of the veterans to Congress for action. They hope to see other states join them as the years go by.

Another state accomplishment: West Virginia recently completed a study of more than 1,200 of its 29,000 Vietnam veterans. The study noted a higher than normal incidence of cancer among them. Seen were three types of cancer, soft tissue sarcoma among them.

Because of these works and others that will take shape in the future, the question of Agent Orange's dangers to all who have been exposed to it—from Vietnam veterans to factory employees and accident victims—may one day be answered. At the moment, however, the herbicide continues to be what it has always been: a sad and mysterious legacy of the Vietnam War.

THE LEGAL BATTLE

In 1978, a veteran named Paul Reutershan brought a lawsuit against the chemical companies that had manufactured Agent Orange for use in Vietnam. Reutershan asked for $10 million in damages for the ills he had suffered in the years following his exposure to the herbicide. His case never went to court, however. Reutershan died just five months after launching the suit.[7]

Soon after his death, the families of five other veterans took up the legal battle. They instituted a class action lawsuit against the companies.[8] The term *class action* means that their suit was launched on behalf of all the veterans who claimed to have suffered the ill effects of Agent Orange. In time, more than 20,000 other veterans joined them in pursuing the action.

The suit was directed against seven chemical companies: Dow Chemical Company, Monsanto Company, Diamond Shamrock Company, Hercules Incorporated, Uniroyal Corporation, T-H Agricultural and Nutrition Company, and Thompson Chemical Company. In the years since the suit was initiated, Thompson has gone out of business.

The veterans believed the government to be primarily responsible for their problems because it was the entity that had ordered

Vietnam vet James Burdge of Long Branch, New Jersey, shows a rash on his arms that he attributes to exposure to Agent Orange.

/ 80 /

the use of Agent Orange in Vietnam. But they felt it would be impossible to sue the government because of a U.S. Supreme Court case back in 1950. In that case, the Court had declared that the government cannot be held liable for injuries suffered by service personnel while on duty.

And so the veterans chose the companies as their targets. They charged that the seven manufacturers had been negligent in making and selling Agent Orange to the government. They argued that the companies should have taken the care to warn users of the dangers posed by the herbicide's dioxin content.

The companies defended themselves by saying that Agent Orange had harmed no one and had never been proven to be the cause of the veterans' problems. They said that they had merely manufactured the defoliant according to the government's specifications.

A Settlement

The case was set for trial in early May 1984, in the U.S. federal court in Brooklyn, New York. But the two opposing sides reached an out-of-court settlement on the weekend before the trial was scheduled to begin. Although both sides insisted that they had enough evidence to win the case, they agreed to the settlement as a way of avoiding a complex and costly trial that promised to drag on for years.

In signing the agreement, the companies made it clear that they were not admitting to any guilt in the matter. The agreement called for them to place $180 million in a trust fund that would then be distributed among all veterans claiming harm by Agent Orange. The fund, which would collect interest at the rate of $61,000 a day, was expected to last for twenty-five years. Estimates held that it could eventually result in payments totaling $750 million.

Although the attorneys on both sides expressed satisfaction with the settlement, the same could not be said of all the people involved in the case. Some veterans thought the amount in the fund to be too small and said that, in light of the profits made from the herbicide's manufacture, the companies had "gotten off the hook" too cheaply. Many corporate executives complained that the settlement exacted an unjustified payment from the companies. Both the veterans and the firms agreed that the suit had been directed at the wrong targets because of the 1950 U.S. Supreme Court decision. The government was at fault and should be made to admit its guilt and work out a scheme of compensation for the Agent Orange victims.

Despite the settlement, the money was not paid out immediately to those claiming Agent Orange damage. Several years passed while a distribution plan was developed and legal questions concerning the fund were explored. It was not until mid-1988 that a final plan for the distribution of the fund took shape.

The Final Distribution Plan

The distribution plan calls for the fund, which had grown to $240 million by mid-1988, to be divided into several categories for distribution. First, there is to be a program in which $170 million in cash benefits will be paid to long-term, totally disabled veterans and to the families of veterans whose deaths are believed to have been linked to Agent Orange. Next, there is to be a $52 million program to finance social service projects that benefit veterans and their families.

Another $5 million is planned for distribution to veterans in Australia and New Zealand. Finally, $13 million is to be set aside to pay the attorneys who represented the veterans in the class action suit and to pay the costs of administering the distribution plan.

The fund was to begin making payments in early 1989. A payment of $4.4 million was made to Australia and New Zealand in July 1988.

At the time this book is being written, Congress is considering a measure that will, in part, provide benefits for those veterans who seem to have suffered from exposure to Agent Orange. Under consideration for enactment into law is a bill that will establish financial aid and other types of help for all eligible veterans, among them the victims of the legacy called Agent Orange.

THE FOURTH LEGACY

THE LOST AMERICANS

CHAPTER
SEVEN
MISSING
IN ACTION

We turn now from the legacies bequeathed to the veterans and look at a terrible gift left to a number of U.S. families. They are the families of the service personnel and civilians who went to Vietnam and were never seen again. Their loved ones are listed as missing in action (MIA).

THE MIA/POW LIST

When the Paris peace pact was signed in 1973, the U.S. Department of Defense published a list of over 3,100 names. The names were those of Americans designated as either MIA or POW (prisoners of war). The signing of the pact was followed by an exchange of prisoners between the United States and North Vietnam. Returned to U.S. hands at the time were approximately 600 men.[1]

Their names were removed from the MIA/POW list, reducing its total to just over 2,500 names. Those remaining names were of soldiers, sailors, airmen, and civilians who had disappeared in various ways, never to be seen again. Some had vanished in battle.

Some had disappeared when their aircraft crashed into jungle areas or the sea. Some were thought to have been captured but had not been returned in the U.S.-Vietnamese prisoner exchange. They all became known as MIAs. Included in their number were two women and forty-two civilian workers.

Not all the MIAs had been lost in Vietnam itself. Several hundred had vanished in neighboring countries—some 556 in Laos, 82 in Cambodia (Kampuchea), and 2 in China. Counted as lost in North and South Vietnam—and in the sea off their coasts—were approximately 1,800 servicemen.[2]

The People on the List

Many on the Department of Defense MIA/POW list were thought to be dead because they had disappeared in such violent circumstances as artillery barrages and air crashes. They were designated as missing because their bodies had never been recovered. It only *seemed* certain that they were dead. But there was no solid proof of their deaths—and would not be until their bodies or bits of their shattered bodies were located and identified.

For example, the list contained the names of thirteen men who had been aboard an AC-130 gunship on a night in December 1972. While returning to its base in Thailand after a mission above North Vietnam, the aircraft was hit by enemy antiaircraft fire. Although its fuel line was punctured, it managed to stay aloft until it was over a jungle area in Laos. Then it suddenly exploded and plunged earthward. Two crewmen parachuted to safety, but fourteen of their comrades failed to follow them out. The AC-130 crashed in a giant cloud of fire and smoke. A rescue team made its way to the crash site the following day and found the remains of one man. The other crewmen, thirteen in all, were thought to be incinerated and

Metal caskets containing what were believed to be the remains of MIAs, arranged in rows on a runway in Hawaii

buried deep in the wreckage. Although it seemed certain that they were all dead, the rescue team could not be absolutely sure that no one had survived to be captured by the enemy. The thirteen were listed as MIAs.[3]

Also on the list were men who were thought to have been captured at the time of their disappearance. Among them were an Air Force pilot and his copilot. In 1973, they ejected from their observation plane when enemy fire brought it down in South Vietnam. Both were sighted from the air as their parachutes floated to earth. On landing, one of the men radioed that enemy troops were approaching and would surely take him captive. The pilot and his copilot were never seen again.[4]

Finally, there were men on the list who were definitely known to have been captured. One was an Army staff sergeant who was accompanying a South Vietnamese army unit on a patrol of enemy territory in 1967. When shots suddenly rang out from the surrounding underbrush, the sergeant dropped to the ground with a bullet in his leg. His companions retreated and then watched as four North Vietnamese soldiers came out of the underbrush and led him away. The sergeant was not among the Americans who were returned in the U.S.-Vietnamese prisoner exchange and has not been seen to this day.

A PUBLIC OUTCRY

The disappearance of more than 2,500 Americans triggered an outcry throughout the United States. The families of the missing men, along with concerned fellow citizens everywhere, demanded to know what had happened to them. They wanted to know if any of the missing were still alive and being held captive by the Vietnamese; if so, they wanted the U.S. government to locate them and bring them home. They wanted to know if the remains of any of the men thought to be dead had been found by the Vietnamese; if so, they wanted them retrieved and brought home for proper burial. The families and friends of those thought to be dead wanted to know if their loved ones had actually perished. Only when they learned for sure could they be free of the anguish of not knowing the fate of a loved one. Only then could they get on with their lives.

Unique in American History

Not only was the outcry widespread, but it was also considered unique in American history. Greater numbers of men had been lost in World War II and Korea—78,751 in World War II and 8,177 in Korea—but there had been no large-scale public demand that they be found.[5] Why? In great part, the answer is that these two earlier wars were supported by most Americans and seen as necessary conflicts. People mourned the lost men, but were resigned to thinking of them as part of the costs that had to be borne in fighting necessary wars.

Such was not the case with the Vietnam War. With the U.S. role in the fighting strongly opposed by many, if not most, Americans, it was a war that spread deep feelings of guilt throughout the country. Added was an equally deep sense of shame when everything ended in defeat. In the eyes of many Americans, the nation had lost its honor. For them, as journalist James Rosenthal wrote in a 1985 issue of *New Republic* magazine, the finding of the MIAs and their return were matters connected with restoring the nation's honor.[6]

No matter what prompted it, the outcry has proven to be an unending one. It is still with us today. And so is the search for the MIAs, both living and dead. It continues today, long years after it started in 1973.

THE BEGINNING SEARCH

The Paris peace pact contained twenty-three agreements that were to be observed by the warring sides (called *parties* in the agreements) when the fighting stopped. One of those agreements concerned the MIAs. It stipulated that

> *The parties shall help each other to get information about those military personnel and foreign civilians of the par-*

/ 91 /

ties missing in action, to determine the location and take care of the graves of the dead so as to facilitate the exhumation and repatriation of the remains.[7]

Work on this agreement began immediately after the pact was signed. A joint military team, which consisted of members from both sides, took shape. Its task was to discuss the living and dead MIAs and to exchange information that could pave the way to their recovery.[8]

The team members on both sides expected trouble because the angers of the war still blazed hot and because of the fear that the United States and Vietnam would run into difficulties with each other over honoring the many agreements in the peace pact. But the team's work got off to a smooth start. The North Vietnamese members told the U.S. members that they looked on the finding of the missing as a "humanitarian issue" meant to end the suffering of so many American families. They said that the work on the MIAs must not be harmed in any way by the problems that might arise between the United States and Vietnam over the peace pact agreements.

The North Vietnamese members followed their words with actions. They arranged for the return of the bodies of twenty-three dead U.S. servicemen. At the same time, they granted permission for U.S. search parties to visit known air crash sites in South Vietnam with an eye to finding and identifying the remains of the victims. They permitted eighteen searches to be conducted between May and December 1973. Located were the remains of nine missing Americans. Seven of that number were airmen who had disappeared back in 1969. Their remains were found where their helicopter had crashed in a dense jungle area some 200 miles northeast of Saigon.*

---

*A principal agreement in the peace pact stipulated that the United States must not interfere in the affairs of Vietnam. Consequently, the U.S. members of the joint military team had to obtain North Vietnamese permission before conducting any searches.

Within weeks of getting off to such a good start, the team ran into trouble. It was caused by the very factors that the North Vietnamese members had said must never intrude on the team's efforts—disagreements between the U.S. and Vietnam over the peace pact agreements. Both sides angrily accused each other of violating the agreements in various ways. The anger caused by the accusations trickled down to the team. The North Vietnamese members became increasingly uncooperative. They stopped providing the U.S. members with MIA information. They began to forbid or ignore all American requests to make searches of air crash sites.

And there was another problem. It was one that caused the American team members to charge that the MIA work was being damaged by what they called "economic blackmail."

"Economic Blackmail"

This charge stemmed from a provision in the peace pact that called for the United States to provide economic aid to help the North Vietnamese recover from the war.9 Soon after the pact was signed, President Richard Nixon sent a letter to North Vietnam's prime minister. In it, he estimated that the aid would add up to about $3.5 billion. The North Vietnamese looked on Mr. Nixon's statement as an outright promise of that amount, even though they were warned by U.S. officials that the funds could not be awarded without the consent of Congress.

Consequently, the North Vietnamese thought themselves being cheated when Mr. Nixon began to place restrictions on the awarding of the funds. One was that the money would not be forthcoming until the troubled joint military team once again began to make progress in its MIA work. The North Vietnamese members reacted angrily. The MIA work slowed even more.

The team's American members contended that their North Vietnamese counterparts were stalling the MIA work until Mr. Nixon's promised aid came through. This was, they charged, "economic blackmail." On the opposite side of the fence, the North Vietnamese said that the President had cheated them by promising the aid and then attaching certain restrictions. In all, the battle over

/ 93 /

the proposed aid and the accusations of peace pact violations by both the United States and Vietnam led to the downfall of the joint military team. It disbanded in 1974.[10]

ACTIONS IN THE UNITED STATES

While things were falling apart for the joint military team, the demand that the lost Americans—especially those who might still be alive and imprisoned by the North Vietnamese—be found remained strong in the U.S. President Gerald R. Ford, who took office in 1974, responded to the demand by asking that a group of ten congressmen be assigned to study the MIA/POW problem. In September 1975, the House Select Committee on Missing Persons in Southeast Asia was formed.[11]

The committee spent fifteen months at its task. In that time, it reviewed the files on some 200 missing service personnel, studied 100 documents pertaining to MIAs and POWs, and traveled to Hanoi to speak with North Vietnamese officials. Then, in late 1976, the committee chairman, Representative G. V. "Sonny" Montgomery of Mississippi, announced the results of the group's work. The committee, he told the nation, had found that "no Americans are being held alive as prisoners" by the Vietnamese. He added: "The sad conclusion is that there is no evidence that . . . missing Americans are still alive."

Anger and Doubt

Montgomery's words were met with anger and doubt across the country. His report was called *his* version of the committee's findings rather than a report of what the group actually believed. A widespread public suspicion at the time was that the U.S. government wanted to be rid of the MIA/POW issue. People everywhere felt that Montgomery, backed only by certain members of the committee, was cooperating with the government in this desire.

But a question must be asked here. Why should people suspect their government of wanting to be rid of the MIA/POW issue? The critics of the Montgomery report gave two answers. First, they held that the government wanted to get the issue out of the way as a means of helping put a hated war quickly into the past. If the American people could be made to think that there were no living MIAs being held prisoner, it would help them begin to forget the awful divisiveness that the war had created throughout the nation. A continuing cry for the recovery of living prisoners would only keep the terrible memories of the war alive for years to come.

Second, they argued that the government, while not wanting to pay former President Nixon's proffered \$3.5 billion in aid (in the end, that aid was indeed never paid), did desire to establish good relations and diplomatic ties with the new Vietnamese government. In so doing, it hoped to restore political stability in Southeast Asia. And, economically, it hoped to take advantage of certain benefits that Vietnam had to offer—a principal one being the rich oil deposits lying off its coasts. The MIA/POW problem promised to be a roadblock along the way to the establishment of good relations between the two nations.

Among the most vehement critics of the Montgomery report was the National League of Families of American Missing and Prisoners in Southeast Asia (NLF), a nationwide organization that had been formed in 1970 to learn the status of all MIAs and POWs and to urge the continuing search for them. Its charges against the report were many. A main one held that, although the committee had been in business for fifteen months, it had spent only six months at its work. The rest of the time had been devoted to the formation of a staff for the committee and to leaves of absence taken by the members for vacations and political campaigning. The NLF said that the committee had not given enough time to its actual work to have come up with a competent report.[12]

And there was trouble inside the committee.[13] Five members—fully half the committee's manpower—issued a report in which they claimed that their own findings had indicated there was good reason to think that living MIAs were still being held in Vietnam and the neighboring countries of Laos and Cambodia. The report urged the government to continue looking for them.

The five committee members sent their report to newly elected President Jimmy Carter in 1977. After reviewing it and the Mont-

/ 95 /

gomery report, Mr. Carter opted in favor of the latter. Agreeing that no living Americans were being held in Vietnam and elsewhere, he said that the U.S. would now concentrate its efforts on recovering the remains of the dead MIAs in enemy hands.

President Carter and the MIAs

Mr. Carter's decision brought another nationwide burst of suspicion. Many people said that the President was trying a new strategy in an effort to be rid of the MIA/POW problem. He was attempting to stop a work that the government saw as dangerous to the establishment of good relations with Vietnam. U.S. charges that the former enemy was heartlessly holding Americans captive long after the fighting had ended were bound to delay matters by angering and insulting the Vietnamese. It was far safer to ask that the missing dead be found.

The President followed his approval of the Montgomery report by forming yet another MIA group: the Presidential Commission on America's Missing and Unaccounted for in Southeast Asia.[14] The commission, which was headed by Leonard Woodcock, the former head of the United Auto Workers and later to be the American Ambassador to China, was to visit North Vietnam and negotiate the return of all dead MIAs. The press was soon referring to the group simply as the Woodcock Commission.

The Woodcock Commission traveled to Hanoi in March 1977. After several meetings with Vietnamese officials, the visit ended with Woodcock's announcement that his group agreed with the Montgomery report. There were no living Americans being held by the former enemy. Woodcock went on to say that the Vietnamese government was doing its best to account for the dead MIAs.

Again, there was a burst of public suspicion. Woodcock, like Montgomery, was accused of helping the government be rid of the MIA/POW problem. Fueling the suspicion were news reports that the commission had not been allowed to speak with Vietnamese citizens or to travel outside Hanoi. These prohibitions brought on the belief that Woodcock's group had been kept from gathering information that might have thrown much light on the MIA/POW situation.

There was more trouble for the Carter administration when, in 1978, the Department of Defense declared all the missing men to be "presumed dead."[15] The department announced that it was taking this step so that the families of the MIAs could receive the financial benefits due them for a deceased relative. But many of the families condemned the step as another strategy to be rid of the MIA/POW issue. Men who were declared dead, they angrily pointed out, were easier for the public to forget than ones whom the government continued to list as possibly alive.*

There has never been any proof that the government was actually trying to shove the MIA issue off to the side. What is known is that Mr. Carter's efforts to get on a good footing with Vietnam eventually came to nothing. They collapsed when his administration became mired in difficulties with Iran. Especially troublesome was the problem of attempting to free the fifty-two Americans who were held captive by the Iranians for fourteen months.

And what is also known is that no one—from Congressman Montgomery to President Carter and Leonard Woodcock—could ever convince great segments of the U.S. public that living Americans were not being held prisoner somewhere in Indochina. Nor could they convince great segments of the public that the Vietnamese were doing their best to help locate and return the dead MIAs.

HOW MANY ARE STILL ALIVE?

To this very day, thousands of Americans remain convinced that there are captive MIAs. But how many may still be alive after all

---

*Only one man was not listed as presumed dead—Air Force Col. Charles E. Shelton. He is listed as MIA as a symbol of all the missing.[16]

the years since the war's end is anybody's guess. Estimates made by people involved in the MIA issue have run from several hundred to as few as six.[17] But perhaps all died long ago. No one knows. Nor, if there are MIAs still living, does anyone know how many are being held captive or are living in Southeast Asia of their own accord, perhaps because they have started families there, perhaps because they want no part of the United States for the part it played in the war.

To date, only one living MIA has come out of Indochina. He is Marine Pfc Robert Garwood, who mysteriously vanished from his unit in 1965 and did not reappear until 1979.[18] Garwood was suspected of being either a deserter or a POW who had cooperated with the enemy. The latter view stemmed from reports of his activities during the war years following his disappearance. According to the reports, he had led Vietcong guerrillas against U.S. troops, had shouted communist propaganda at American captives, and had physically and verbally abused a number of the prisoners. When he returned to the United States of his own volition, the Hanoi government announced that he had lived among the North Vietnamese of his own accord.

On his arrival home, Garwood was taken into custody by the Marine Corps and placed on trial. The trial found him guilty of collaborating with the enemy but innocent of desertion.

Garwood said little during his trial but later told the press that he had seen U.S. prisoners in Vietnam after the war's end. He claimed that they had been kept in four prison camps near Hanoi. Two of the camps, he said, had held between forty and sixty men each; each of the other two had housed from six to eight POWs. Some Americans refused to believe his claims, saying that he was

Marine Pfc Robert Garwood is the only living MIA to come out of Indochina. In 1981, he was court-martialed for collaborating with the enemy.

/ 98 /

mentally unbalanced after staying away so long. Other Americans felt that he was telling the truth. Perhaps there will one day be solid evidence to show whether he was lying or telling the truth.

HOW MANY ARE DEAD?

The Vietnamese have returned the remains of some 200 men over the years since the joint military team was at work. Yet, thousands of Americans today are certain that there are many more bodies still to be returned and that the North Vietnamese know about them but are continuing to block their recovery. The feeling remains that the Vietnamese are holding them as hostages for "economic blackmail" or out of hatred for the U.S. role in the war. But how many of our dead are being withheld? Again, as in the case of the possibly still-living MIAs, no one can say for sure, but the suspicion is that the number ranges up into the hundreds.

With so many Americans feeling as they do, the nation's quest to locate its MIAs, both living and dead, has been pursued from the end of the war to the present. It is a quest in which success, failure, sorrow, frustration, and suspicion have all been mixed together.

CHAPTER

EIGHT

THE QUEST FOR
THE MISSING

To make the story of the quest for the MIAs easier to follow, we must separate the searches for the living and the dead and then look at each individually.

THE QUEST
FOR THE LIVING

Why do so many Americans refuse to believe that no living MIAs are being held prisoner by the former enemy? In great part, their disbelief is based on news stories of living Americans being sighted in Southeast Asia.

Reports of the sightings date back to 1975, the year that saw the war finally end with the North Vietnamese capture of South Vietnam's capital city, Saigon. The reports have grown swiftly through the years. Word of 486 sightings reached the United States by 1983. The number vaulted to 3,508 by the end of 1985. The total sightings stand at over 7,100 at the time this book is being written.[1]

You may wonder why the number of sightings have increased so dramatically over the years. The answer is that, ever since 1976, word of them has come from the countless refugees who have fled Vietnam, Laos, and Cambodia. Although the war ended in 1975, the subsequent years were so crowded with troubles for the three countries that a mass exodus over their borders resulted.

Take what happened when Saigon fell. Thousands of citizens who had supported the South Vietnamese government or had fought in its army fled to avoid reprisals by the victorious Northerners. As for Laos and Cambodia, years of political and military strife have plagued both countries, driving multitudes of their people to flight. Many of the refugees made their way to nearby Thailand, where huge camps were set up to house them while they waited to return home when peace was restored or to emigrate to a foreign country, often the United States. At times, the camps have housed as many as a quarter of a million people.

A great many sightings were reported by the Laotians while they were in the Thai camps or after they had traveled to the United States. For example, a Laotian military pilot who made his way to freedom in 1980 said that he had spent eighteen years in a communist prison. He claimed to have had a number of Americans as cellmates during that time. He estimated that between forty and fifty Americans were being held captive in Laos seven long years after the war had ended.[2]

Some reports came from Vietnamese refugees. Among these refugees was a doctor who claimed that he had treated a number of wounded American prisoners during the war years.[3]

Official Doubts

Although the reported sightings have been many, they have always been the target of a serious question. Can they be trusted as accurate? The answer is that some appear to be accurate. The vast majority, however, have been greeted with doubt by U.S. officials.

The officials have reasons for their skepticism.[4] First, they point out that many of the refugees may have been lying. Those who made their way to America may have dreamed up their reports in the hopes that the U.S. government would show its appreciation by helping them financially or in other ways as they began life in their new country. Likewise, the refugees who had yet to leave the Thai camps may have concocted sightings with the aim of having an appreciative American government give them something as simple as extra food or something so vital as assistance in entering the United States.

Another reason for doubt: Many reports have been too vague in their descriptions of the sighted MIAs for U.S. officials to take seriously. Some reports, for example, have been of men who were described as Americans simply because they were white. They just as easily could have been Europeans who were in Vietnamese hands for one reason or another.

Still another reason: Many reports have turned out not to be of firsthand sightings. The refugees reporting them did not actually see an MIA. Rather, they only heard of him from someone else. These reports have always been dismissed as being hearsay and are considered worthless.

In light of these varied doubts, how many sightings can be judged to be of value? For the answer, we must turn to the Defense Intelligence Agency (DIA). The DIA is a branch of the Department of Defense and is the organization responsible for receiving and evaluating all reported sightings of live MIAs.[5]

The Defense Intelligence Agency at Work

The backbone of the DIA is its system of computers. The computers contain data on all the sightings reported over the years, plus other needed information. The additional information includes the names of MIAs whose fates have already been determined. Among them are men known to be dead because their remains have been returned through the years by the Vietnamese. Also included in the additional material are satellite and aerial photographs of air crash sites.

Whenever a new sighting is reported, the information on it goes into the computers to be compared with the already stored

/ 103 /

data in several ways. For example, let's say that a refugee today reports that he sighted a living MIA in the mid-1970s. His description of the MIA will be fed into the computers and matched with those of all reported MIAs. It may end up matching the description of an MIA sighting that was found to be a fabrication. Or it may end up matching the description of an MIA whose fate is already known to the DIA. In either instance, the DIA will close the case and declare the sighting to be "resolved."

In addition to working with its computer system, the DIA interviews all people who report sightings. The principal aims here are to learn if the report is of a firsthand sighting and to determine that it is a truthful one. If the sighting is not firsthand, it is immediately discarded. To establish the truth of a sighting, the DIA asks the person reporting it to take a polygraph (lie detector) test. The DIA gives the test only if the individual consents to it.

What has the agency accomplished over the years? Of the more than 7,100 reports on hand at the time of this book's writing, it has discounted all but about 1,000 because they were not firsthand sightings. Of that approximate 1,000, the agency has resolved over 870. Some 213 of the resolved cases have been judged to be false, while about 660 have been found to involve MIAs whose fates were already known.

Left are just upwards of 120 sightings that have not been resolved. They remain open for further investigation. Of these unresolved cases, the DIA lists between 65 and 74 as "most compelling." This means they contain certain points of evidence that indicate the Vietnamese know more about the sighted MIAs than they have thus far admitted. But this does not necessarily mean that these men are still alive after all the years that have passed since the war. They may be alive, yes. Or they may be dead. Who can say?

The DIA Under Fire

Over the years, the DIA has run into several criticisms for the way it carries out its work.[6] One often-heard complaint is directed at the high number of discounted and resolved cases. Many people do not trust this number, saying it indicates that the agency is cooperating in what they suspect to be the government's continuing effort to be rid of the MIA issue; it is easier, they contend, to make the public forget these cases than unresolved ones. Others do not agree with this stand, but feel that the DIA follows a set of unwise policies in its work.

A basic criticism of DIA policy contends that the agency does not trust a refugee's report by itself. Before taking any report seriously, the agency wants to see it supported by other evidence. For example, suppose that someone claims to have sighted Americans in a jungle prison camp. The DIA wants to see satellite or aerial photographs of the camp to know that it actually exists. If there is no such evidence at hand, the agency is inclined to dismiss the report as useless.

There is widespread belief that this policy and others like it have prompted the DIA to turn away too quickly from many reported sightings. Further investigation of these reports might have yielded valuable information on living Americans still in Indochina.

In all, despite the DIA's resolved cases, the more than 7,100 sightings through the years have made it impossible for many Americans to think that not one of their countrymen is still living among the enemy either as a prisoner or of his own free will.

THE QUEST
FOR THE DEAD

The American public has long had to face a sad fact about the MIAs thought to have died in the war. The bodies of many, if not most, will never be located and recovered because the men were torn to bits in such tragedies as air crashes and artillery barrages. Their remains, along with those of the men who disappeared in dense jungle growth, are simply impossible to find.

But there is much evidence to support the widely held suspicion that the Vietnamese know the whereabouts of many MIA remains and are refusing to return them to the United States, hoping either to trade them for the $3.5 billion in aid proffered by President Nixon or to win some other economic or political advantage. For example, there is the report of a Vietnamese mortician who made his way to freedom in the late 1970s. He claimed to have once seen the bodies of more than 400 Americans. They were stored on racks in a warehouse in Hanoi.[7]

And there is a remark that was made in 1973 by a Vietnamese member of the joint military team. As quoted in the book *Without Honor* by journalist Arnold R. Isaacs, the Vietnamese told an American team member that Vietnam held the remains of many American soldiers and airmen. He said that his country did not like to have these men and that their graves were an insult to his homeland and an awful reminder of the damage that the U.S. had done in Vietnam. He finished with the statement that Vietnam wanted to return these men but saw no reason to do so just because the Americans were asking for them.[8]

There is also evidence to show that the Vietnamese have lied to the United States about the dead MIAs. Throughout the years, when the U.S. has asked about certain MIAs, the Vietnamese have often claimed to know nothing about them—only to belie this claim by later returning their remains. A case in point here concerns a Navy flier who was shot down in 1967. The North Vietnamese immediately announced on radio that he had survived and had been captured. Later, they used him in a propaganda film. But, for years, whenever the U.S. asked after the man's fate, the Vietnamese denied any knowledge of him. Then they returned his remains in 1981—without a word of explanation.[9]

Is it possible that they knew nothing about the flier through all the years between 1967 and 1981? It hardly seems likely, not after broadcasting his capture and then using him in a propaganda film.

But what of the dead MIAs who have been returned? Let us turn to them now.

The Returned Americans

As you'll recall from Chapter Seven, the Vietnamese returned twenty-three sets of remains and permitted the search of an air crash site that yielded nine more sets during the months when the joint military team was at work. The passing years, despite the collapse of the team and despite the problems that have beset the U.S. and Vietnam, have seen the return of additional remains.

The term "sets of remains" is used here rather than "bodies" for a reason. Most of the dead men have not been returned with their bodies intact. Rather, bits of their bones and teeth have been received. This is because, as you know, so many were torn apart in artillery barrages and air crashes. Many others were returned after the years had caused their bodies to decompose.

More than 200 sets have come into U.S. hands since the war's end.[10] Some have been released by the Vietnamese and some have been located by the few U.S. search parties that have been permitted to visit air crash sites. On being returned, the collections of bone and teeth have been sent to the Army's Central Identification Laboratory (CIL) in Hawaii. The laboratory has studied them and, by comparing them with such factors as the height, weight, and age of the many MIAs, has attempted to identify them as belonging to specific men. It claims to have made more than 170 positive identifications.

There is an interesting pattern to be seen in the returns.[11] Some years have seen the remains handed over to the U.S. in fairly large numbers. Other years have produced as few as one to three sets. The pattern is interesting because it reflects the state of relations between the United States and Vietnam. Those relations have never been good, but there have been times when they seemed to be improving. The number of returns has always gone up at those times.

To begin with, there were those twenty-three sets that were returned (plus the nine found at a crash site) when the work of the joint military team was going well. The number of returns fell off dramatically when the team ran into the troubles that eventually saw it disbanded. But the number rose in 1977 when President Carter attempted to establish normal relations with Vietnam; there were sufficient returns for the CIL to claim thirty-three positive identifications that year. When Mr. Carter's efforts came to naught, the number immediately dropped. There were not enough returns for the CIL to claim even one positive identification in 1979.*

The greatest number of returns were seen in the 1980s, during the years of President Ronald Reagan's administration. Sufficient sets of remains were returned for the CIL to announce close to 100 identifications. Two basic reasons accounted for the increase.

THE QUEST FOR THE LIVING: THE 1980s

President Reagan showed a deep interest in the MIAs. He pledged that his administration would give the "highest priority" to the search for the MIAs, both the dead and the possibly still-living. In keeping with that pledge, he sent a delegation to Hanoi in 1982 to discuss the MIA issue with Vietnamese officials. The result was the formation of a U.S.-Vietnamese committee that met to exchange MIA information and pave the way for the return of the missing dead. At the same time, work was done with Laos to retrieve the MIAs who had been lost there. [12]

*There is a reason for saying that the CIL *claimed* to make positive identifications rather than simply reporting that the laboratory made them. In the mid-1980s, the methods it employed in making identifications came under suspicion. The laboratory was investigated by a team of scientists and its methods were found to be scientifically unsound. As a result, the validity of its identifications through the years was placed in serious doubt.

The outcome of the investigation caused many people to think that the CIL, because it is operated by the military, was making careless and inept identifications as part of the government's suspected desire to be rid of the MIA issue as quickly as possible. Such does not seem to have been the case. The questioned methods of identification had been developed by the lab's chief scientist and, though branded unsound, had been pursued in good faith and not as part of any government plot. The government ordered the laboratory to adopt more acceptable methods of identification. For a detailed account of the CIL investigation, see Chapter Seven of the author's book *MIA: Missing in Action* (New York: Franklin Watts, 1989).

In part because of Mr. Reagan's commitment to the MIAs, both Vietnam and Laos displayed a greater interest in the problem. This increased interest bore fruit in 1985, first in Laos and then in Vietnam.

Early that year, the Laotians permitted a U.S. search team to visit a crash site near the city of Pakse. It was here that the AC-130 gunship mentioned in Chapter Seven had crashed in December 1972. Thirteen airmen, you'll recall, were thought to have been incinerated in the fiery crash. The U.S. search team, made up of twelve men, spent two weeks at the site. Assisted by Laotian soldiers, they unearthed upwards of 50,000 bone and teeth fragments. Many of the fragments were no more than pieces of gray ash. When the fragments were returned to the CIL for study, the laboratory announced that it had positively identified all thirteen victims.*13

The Laotians permitted a second search in 1986. This time, a U.S. team visited a crash site in a jungle area near the city of Savannakhet. Here, another AC-130 gunship had crashed after being hit by enemy fire while on a reconnaissance mission near the border between Laos and Vietnam. Fourteen men had gone down with the aircraft. The visit to the site lasted ten days and yielded some 5,000 bone and teeth fragments, plus such personal gear as sidearms, knives, and dog tags. The fragments netted eight identifications from the CIL. The remaining six victims could not be identified.14

---

*The families of two of the Pakse crash victims were in great part responsible for the investigation into the methods of identification used by the CIL. On learning that the remains of their loved ones consisted of just a handful of tiny bone fragments, they wondered if it was possible to make definite identifications on the basis of such scant evidence. They employed a noted forensic scientist to study the fragments. He reported that, for a variety of technical reasons, the bones were too small to have yielded positive identifications and that the lab's methods of identification were scientifically unsound. His report—and that of a scientist who checked the remains of another returned MIA—led to the investigation of the laboratory.

As important as these searches were, they could not match in significance an announcement from Vietnam in July 1985. The Hanoi government said that, after years of problems with the United States, it wanted to "accelerate" work on the MIA issue and resolve the whole matter in two years' time. A month later, the Vietnamese demonstrated that they meant what they said. They returned twenty-six sets of remains to the U.S. The sets were the most ever returned at one time since the end of the war.[15]

Then, in late 1985, the Vietnamese allowed a U.S. search team to visit the spot where a B-29 bomber had crashed some nine miles from Hanoi in 1972. Found at the site was a small collection of bone fragments. After studying them, the CIL announced that it could not identify them as belonging to specific crewmen because the fragments were too small.[16]

Laotian and Vietnamese Economic Needs

You'll recall that we said there were two reasons for the increased number of returns in the 1980s and that President Reagan's interest in the MIA issue was only in part responsible for that increase. We come now to the second reason. It has to do with the economic situation in Vietnam and Laos.

The economies of both countries were deeply troubled throughout the 1980s. The Laotian economy suffered an especially hard blow in 1984 when the country produced a poor rice crop. The United States helped the Laotians recover by giving them 5,000 tons of rice. Many U.S. officials felt that the Laotian permission to search the Pakse crash site was a thank-you for the donated rice. The timing of the permit certainly gave substance to this view because the United States had been negotiating for permission to make the search since 1982, but to no avail. The officials also suspected that the Laotians were attempting to open the door to improved relations with the U.S. and to the possibility of further American aid.[17]

Vietnam's economic plight can be called a legacy left by the war.[18] It has persisted ever since the fighting ended, even though

/ 110 /

the nation has been receiving foreign aid for years now. The problem is that the aid has not been of the sort that contributes to the building of a strong economy. In the main, it has come from the Soviet Union and has consisted of military supplies and equipment. Not included has been the aid necessary for economic growth, such as consumer goods and technological assistance. As a result, Vietnam has been forced to purchase the needed goods and assistance elsewhere. It has gone deeply into debt in doing so.

The situation eventually led Vietnam to need American aid. Despite President Carter's efforts to normalize U.S.-Vietnamese relations in the late 1970s and despite American fact-finding visits to Vietnam through the years to discuss the MIA problem and other matters, no actual diplomatic ties between Washington and Hanoi had ever been forged. Hence, the sudden Vietnamese cooperation in the MIA quest during the 1980s was seen as a strategy for bringing about the normalization of relations with America. Normal relations would open the way to the diplomatic ties that, in their turn, would make possible the receipt of aid not only from the U.S. but also from a number of other countries friendly to the United States.

Trouble for the Quest

Despite Vietnam's increased cooperation, the 1980s quest for the MIAs did not go smoothly. Causing the trouble were Vietnam's relations with its neighbor, Cambodia.

During the war years, Vietnam exerted much influence over Cambodia.[19] In 1975, however, the Cambodian political faction known as the Khmer Rouge took control of the country, establishing a cruel regime that forced countless people to flee the nation. Its leaders rebelled against the hated Vietnamese influence. The rebellion saw them engage in a number of skirmishes over lands along the Cambodian-Vietnamese border.

In 1978, Vietnam launched a campaign to regain control of Cambodia. It was a campaign that ended in success when invading troops captured Phnom Penh, the nation's capital. Quickly placed in power was a group of men who had broken away from the Khmer Rouge and were sympathetic to Vietnam. They gave the country a new name—the People's Republic of Kampuchea.*

In the years that followed, the Khmer Rouge and its supporters fought to overthrow the Vietnamese-backed government and to oust the Vietnamese troops that were protecting it.

But what does all this have to do with the quest for the MIAs? The connection is this: While Vietnam was intensifying its MIA efforts in the 1980s as a means of hastening a normalization of relations with America, the Reagan administration was insisting that normalization could not come until there was a political settlement in Cambodia. By "political settlement," Mr. Reagan meant that Vietnam must pull its troops out of Cambodia and let the country go its own way.

This insistence caused tensions that slowed the progress toward a resolution of the MIA problem. But it finally began to pay dividends. In 1988, Vietnam announced that it was planning to leave Cambodia.[20] The move was viewed not only as a way of drawing closer to normal relations with the U.S. but also as an escape from a situation that had become a painful burden. The costs of supporting the Cambodian-based troops had been great. So had the costs in life, with the Vietnamese losing some 25,000 men in the years of the Cambodian strife. Their withdrawal plan called for the departure of 50,000 troops in 1988. All were to be gone by 1990.

The announcement of the withdrawal promised to hasten an end to the MIA problem. In July 1988, the United States and Vietnam announced plans to launch a joint mission to recover the remains of still-missing servicemen. The search was also expected to include MIAs possibly still alive—the sixty-five to seventy-four "most compelling" MIA cases that were discussed earlier in this chapter.

---

*Although its formal name is Kampuchea, we are referring to the country as Cambodia in this book because many nations have refused to recognize the new name and because, of the two, Cambodia is the more familiar.

/ 112 /

But the plan quickly ran into trouble. In early August, Vietnam canceled the mission. The Hanoi government, in an angry statement, gave as its reason "the hostile policy" of the Reagan administration.

Behind the cancellation was a remark by an administration official. He triggered Hanoi's rage when he came out against a proposed resolution by the U.S. Congress to establish beginning diplomatic ties now that Vietnamese troops were being removed from Cambodia. He argued that no relations of any sort should be established with Vietnam until the troop withdrawal was completed in 1990.

Hanoi's decision to abandon the joint mission, however, proved to be a temporary one. With its desire for the establishment of normal relations with the U.S. obviously overriding its anger, the Vietnamese government announced that it would resume work on the joint effort to find the still-missing Americans. Additionally, in 1989, the Laotian government and the United States agreed to work together year-round on searches and air-crash site excavations to determine the fates of the more than 500 American servicemen listed as missing in Laos.[21]

At the time this book is being written, the joint efforts with both Vietnam and Laos to find the MIAs and return them home are under way. To be located are just upwards of 2,400 Americans still unaccounted for in Indochina after more than fifteen long years. The hope runs high that all who are not beyond discovery will be located and brought home. Perhaps then, one of the saddest legacies of the Vietnam War will finally be resolved.

THE FIFTH LEGACY

THE FLIGHT TO FREEDOM

CHAPTER

NINE

FLIGHT TO
A NEW LIFE

In the days and then the years that followed the war's end in 1975, thousands of people fled both the southern and northern regions of Vietnam.

Some in South Vietnam left because they had supported or served in the Saigon government or had fought in its armed forces and were fearful of what would happen to them at the hands of the enemy. Others departed because of their religious and political views; they could not tolerate the idea of living in a communist state. And, in both the North and the South, there were many who took flight to avoid the poverty that seemed sure to be their lot as Vietnam struggled to recover from the ravages of the war.

The departing Vietnamese were soon joined by multitudes of Laotians who left their country because of the post-war strife there. Then they found themselves in the midst of thousands more—all the people who fled Cambodia when the brutal Khmer Rouge took over in late 1975. In all, the exodus from the three countries eventually involved close to two million people.

It was an exodus that lasted for years. The fact is that it has continued to this day. Although it began chiefly in fear, it goes on today principally as an escape from the desperate economic conditions in Vietnam, Laos, and Cambodia. It ranks as one of the war's greatest legacies, a legacy that is marked by tragedy, hardship, and hope—tragedy because it has uprooted so many people from their homes, livelihoods, friends, and cultures; hardship because their journeys to freedom were marked always with danger and the threat of death; and hope because the flight has always held out the promise of fresh and successful lives in new lands for all. For many, it is a hope that has become a reality.

TO NEW LANDS

In its early days, the flight to freedom took the Vietnamese, Laotian, and Cambodian escapees to such places as Malaysia, Singapore, Thailand, Guam, Wake Island, and the Philippine Islands. There, they were placed in refugee camps, some of which grew to gigantic proportions. On arriving in the camps, some refugees expressed the hope that peace would return to their countries one day soon so that they could return home. Most, however, knew that they could never go home again. Their goal was to find new nations in which to begin life afresh.

Due to efforts by the United Nations, the governments of various nations, many private organizations, and countless families and individuals, more than 1.5 million refugees reached their goal and settled in various parts of the world.[1] The greatest number were accepted by four Western nations—the United States, Canada, Australia, and France. To date, the four have taken in 1,154,000 newcomers. That total breaks down as shown on page 120.

Indochinese refugees living in crowded conditions, awaiting resettlement in other countries

/ 118 /

United States	821,000
Canada	116,000
Australia	114,000
France	103,000
Total	1,154,000

The other countries that accepted refugees, Japan among them, took in not more than 25,000 each. An exception here is China. China and Vietnam are nations that have been enemies for centuries. Consequently, when the Vietnamese invaded Cambodia in 1978 and regained control of the country, some 280,000 of the Chinese living there took flight. Traveling overland or by sea, they made their way to China. Most are still living there today, working as farmers, fishermen, merchants, and business people. Some of the escapees came of families that had called Cambodia home for generations. China, with financial assistance from the United Nations, has provided upwards of $155 million through the years to help the refugees. [2]

Of the four Western nations listed above, the United States has opened its doors the widest. It has taken in more than half of the 1.5 million refugees. The U.S. has also been instrumental in urging Canada, Australia, and France to liberalize their immigration policies so that they could accept the refugees in great number. Further, over the years, more than $4.9 billion in federal aid has been allotted to the work of helping the "new Americans" settle themselves in and start life over again. [3]

THE FIRST OF
THE "NEW AMERICANS"

The exodus began when Saigon fell in 1975. [4] As enemy troops closed in on the city for the final kill, approximately 130,000 South Vietnamese took flight. Some were helped on their way by the U.S. forces still in Saigon. Others fled to the nation's coasts, there to buy their way aboard small freighters and all types of coastal boats for a wind- and wave-tossed trip that usually took them to Malaysia, Singapore, or Thailand.

For the most part, the people whom the Americans helped were high-ranking government officials, military officers, and long time workers in government departments. They were placed aboard military air and sea transport and taken to several destinations, chief among them Guam, Wake Island, and the Philippines, where they were processed for entry into America.

The next people to be helped by the U.S. as the war ground to its end were of a more ordinary stripe—common soldiers, small businessmen, merchants, farmers, and fishermen. They, too, were taken to Guam, Wake Island, and the Philippines for processing prior to leaving for the United States. They were joined by the first waves of fleeing Laotians and Cambodians. Processed along with them were approximately 6,000 Cambodians and 7,000 Laotians.

Washington's generosity in opening the nation's door so wide for the first refugees was understandable on several counts. Many refugees had been loyal to the American cause during the war and were owed the best repayment that could be made to them. Many, because of their religious and political beliefs, opposed communism; theirs was an ideological stand that the U.S. government appreciated. Finally, the United States had a long tradition of welcoming the refugees of conflict; the nation had helped thousands who had been uprooted by World War II and by the Hungarian uprising against the Soviet Union in 1956.

But the government's generosity toward the Vietnamese escapees did not sit well with many Americans. Since the U.S. economy was depressed at the time and some nine million workers were unemployed, there was widespread fear that the newcomers would overcrowd the labor market and make work harder for the American jobless to find. There was also the fear that the newcomers would create other problems such as overwhelming the housing market and bringing new diseases into the country.

Mixed with these fears was a cold prejudice on the part of some people. They simply did not want foreigners in their midst. It was an attitude that struck many Americans as anything from ironic to loathsome in light of the fact that, with the exception of the nation's Native American population, the United States was made up totally of foreigners or the children of foreigners.

/ 121 /

Despite the opposition expressed by some segments of the population, the government quickly went about the task of settling the newcomers. The settlement worked so efficiently that most of the 130,000 initial escapees were ready to begin their new lives by the end of 1975. The exodus eased to a trickle for a few months. Then, sometime in 1976, it suddenly regained its strength as the political and economic conditions in Vietnam, Laos, and Cambodia worsened. It turned into the flood that eventually brought 1.5 million Indochinese to new lands.

After welcoming the initial refugees, the United States set limits on the number of Indochinese it could welcome. Refugees could be admitted only if they had families already in the country. Consequently, just as the exodus itself eased for a while, so did the flow of refugees into the nation fall off. But then came the flood tide, which reached its peak in the last years of the 1970s. So great was the exodus by then that the U.S. had to change its policy and permit the entry of an increasing number of refugees. Allowed to enter were 7,000 people a month. In time, the increase saw the United States absorb some 821,000 new citizens.

THE BOAT PEOPLE

Many of the refugees walked overland to freedom. They hiked out of Cambodia and Laos and into neighboring Thailand. There, with U.N. assistance, refugee camps were established. At one time, the Thai camps were housing more than 140,000 people, while another 150,000 were to be found in Cambodian jungle camps next to the Thai border.5

Most refugees from Vietnam, however, attempted to reach freedom via the sea. Traveling in anything from sampans, dories, and Chinese junks to barges, fishing trawlers, and small freighters,

Rescued boat people aboard the French navy's ship Victor Schoelcher *in 1985, awaiting transfer to a refugee camp in the Philippines.*

/ 122 /

they set out for four primary destinations—nearby Malaysia, Singapore, Thailand, and the more distant Hong Kong. Some, however, traveled as far north as Japan and as far south as Australia, journeys that covered thousands of miles. The seagoing refugees soon became known worldwide as "the boat people."

The experiences of the boat people add up to a great drama in which courage, hope, fear, suffering, and outright terror all played a part. Here now are just a few of their stories. The stories are representative of the experiences of all who took to the sea in search of new lives.

The Army Captain

The South Vietnamese army captain was thirty-three years old at the time Saigon fell.[6] Certain that the future held nothing but imprisonment and perhaps torture and death at the hands of the victorious Northerners, he packed a knapsack with food and headed for the southeastern coast. Not having a family to worry about, he was able to leave immediately and travel swiftly. He walked by night and slept concealed in the underbrush by day.

On arriving at the coast, he came upon a group of people trying to launch a thirty-foot open boat. It was an ancient, worm-eaten thing that had been abandoned on the beach by a local fisherman who had now demanded—and received—an outrageous price for its purchase. The captain helped to push the boat into the surf and then climbed aboard with his new companions—ninety in all. Slowly, jammed shoulder to shoulder and taking turns at the oars, they worked the boat down around the southern tip of Vietnam and made their way southwest to Malaysia. Seven people died of starvation during the voyage.

To this day, the captain cannot recall when their supplies ran out or for how long they went without food and water. His guess is that they were without any sustenance whatsoever for more than a week. His chief memory is of the constant fear that the waves would swamp the overburdened vessel and send them all to their deaths. Accompanying it was the fear of being caught in a storm and not knowing how to handle the boat. Only one man aboard, a fisherman, knew anything about sailing.

Neither fear became a reality and the boat reached Thailand safely. Today, the captain is an appliance repairman in northern California. He hopes to open his own repair shop in the near future.

The "Chinese" Family

Unlike the captain, many boat people were not actually escapees. Vietnam's new government allowed them to leave. It did so because it saw them as the customers for a new and highly profitable business, one that eventually involved the equivalent of millions of dollars.[7] They were set free—for a price. That price, which was paid to the authorities in gold, equaled about $3,000 for an adult and $1,500 for a child. The business was not officially sanctioned by the government, but was quietly permitted because it made so many local and national officials wealthy.

The new enterprise was aimed primarily at the wealthy Chinese who were living in both the northern and southern areas of Vietnam. Eager to leave, they gladly paid the price to go aboard overcrowded barges, fishing boats, and small freighters. They were soon joined by Vietnamese who had learned to speak a little Chinese and were able to win their freedom by pretending to be Chinese. Another new business immediately sprang up—the manufacture of false identity papers. It was an underground business that put great wealth into the hands of anyone able to turn out the papers. Again, here was a business that was not officially sanctioned by the government but was condoned because of the profits it brought to so many officials. Those profits came mainly from bribes paid by the "manufacturers" in exchange for not arresting them and closing their shops.

Armed with false papers, countless Vietnamese families were able to leave under the pretense of being Chinese. One such family was made up of four members.[8] Along with 1,400 other people, they were placed on a small ship bound for Hong Kong, a journey that lasted eight days. Those eight days seemed endless. The vessel was so crowded that there was not even room for anyone to sit down. Nor was there food and water aboard. Many of the older people died. Their bodies were tossed overboard by crewmen.

On arrival in Hong Kong, the family was housed in a refugee

camp, remaining there for two months before being sent on to Canada, where they were greeted by a Canadian couple who had agreed to be their sponsors in their new land. The couple took them in and helped them to start life anew.

The family members are now living successful lives in western Canada. The daughter works as a bookkeeper and as an interpreter for the local courts. She also tutors new Vietnamese immigrants in English.

The Thai Pirates

So many boat people attempted to sail from Vietnam to Malaysia, Singapore, and Thailand that yet another new and especially cruel business took shape—piracy.[9] The piracy was carried out by Thai seamen who roamed the seas separating the four countries, constantly attacking the overloaded boats. The pirates robbed the passengers of whatever food and valuables they carried, ripping open suitcases and canvas bags in search of money and jewelry, tearing rings from fingers or, if the rings would not come away easily, cutting off the fingers.

One young Vietnamese woman will never forget the pirates who boarded her boat in 1978. She was one of nine women on board. Not content with robbing the passengers, the marauders forced the women to go to a cabin below decks. There, screaming in pain and terror, the women were raped time and again. Several of the victims, the young woman among them, became pregnant as a result of the attacks. She rejected the idea of having an abortion and planned to travel to the United States after the child's birth. Her parents were already in the U.S. and awaiting her arrival.

The pirates did not stop at robbery and rape. One man recalls that his sixteen-year-old sister and several other women were dragged from his boat and placed aboard the pirate ship at the end of an attack. He never saw her or heard any word of her again. He believes that her fate was the same as that of hundreds of other young women. She was, he says, probably held prisoner for the pleasure of the pirates and then either killed, abandoned, or sold to the operator of a brothel in some Asian port.

An elderly man who is now a fisherman on the southern U.S.

coast left Vietnam aboard a small ship crammed with 350 passengers. Their destination was Malaysia and their journey was supposed to last for two and a half days. Before they arrived, their ship absorbed five pirate attacks. The marauders took the passenger's clothing and money, and raped the women. On two occasions, the pirates ended their strikes by ramming the boat and trying to sink it. After the pirates departed, two Thai fishing boats came on the scene. It was only with their help that the vessel managed to stay afloat and reach port.

At one time, an American official who interviewed refugees landing in Thailand estimated that 30 percent of the boats departing Vietnam were being attacked by the Thai pirates. Later, the United Nations calculated that the women on 81 percent of the attacked boats had been raped.

Constant Companions

Hunger . . . thirst . . . pirate attacks . . . rape . . . death: these were the constant companions of the boat people. No one knows how many refugees died en route to freedom, but the number is thought to be in the thousands. Many escapees, especially the aged and the very young, succumbed to starvation and exposure to the elements. Others were lost when their ships were swamped by the sea or sent to the bottom by pirates. Since the boats stayed close to shore whenever possible, the victims of sinkings often managed to swim ashore, but there were always those who did not know how to swim or had not the strength left to keep themselves afloat. A haunting memory for one woman who now lives in the U.S. is that of her young sister's face as the child went below the waves for the last time after their ship had been destroyed by pirates.[10]

On some ships hunger became so great that the people lost their senses and turned on each other. One man remembers that he was fifteen years old when, by himself, he stole aboard a boat bound for Hong Kong. Food and water soon ran out and starvation took over on a voyage that lasted fifty-two days. The captain ordered a passenger to kill the boy with a hammer so that his body could be eaten. The teenager managed to survive the attack. But the hammer-wielding passenger was found dead the next day. His

/ 127 /

body was cut up and distributed among the passengers in small pieces.[11]

In all fairness to the people whom the refugees encountered, it must be said that the terrors and hardships were often balanced by kindness. The Malaysian people, for example, were noted for their kindness to the new arrivals. They helped them to obtain food and housing, sometimes for a fee, but, as often as not, out of the goodness of their hearts.

Or take the ships of the foreign nations that sighted the boat people at sea. Freighters and liners alike obeyed an age-old rule of the sea and stopped to see if assistance was needed. If a boat was about to sink, the ships took the refugees aboard and carried them to the next port of call. When a boat was able to continue on its own, the ships provisioned it with food and water.[12]

Still another example of kindness: the work done by two Thai fishing vessels to keep a refugee boat afloat after pirates had twice rammed it. The crews of the fishing boats not only saved 350 lives but also risked their own had the pirates learned of what they had done.

AN INTERNATIONAL HELPING HAND

In time, however, the acts of kindness began to disappear. Accounting for their disappearance were the vast numbers of boat people. Such countries as Thailand, Singapore, and Malaysia found the numbers simply too great to handle. The newcomers upset the economies, caused frictions in areas where the religious practices differed from theirs, and put a terrible strain on the food supplies and living space. Many Malaysians, formerly so welcoming, now took to pelting the refugees with rocks whenever boats attempted to land. Singapore adopted a policy of permitting refugees to come ashore only if they could prove that they had relatives in distant lands who would take them quickly. In 1979, the five nations that make up the Association of Southeast Asian Nations (ASEAN)—Thailand, Singapore, Malaysia, Indonesia, and the Philippines—announced that they could no longer allow refugees to land.[13]

The United Nations immediately took steps to ease the plight of the refugees.[14] It brought the representatives of sixty-five nations together for a two-day conference in mid-1979. Out of the meeting came pledges of $190 million to help the boat people. Several Western nations promised to increase the number of wanderers to whom they would grant entry. The United States, which was admitting 7,000 Indochinese per month at the time, raised its monthly quota to 14,000.

Vietnam attended the conference. Its representatives refused to admit that their country was sanctioning the business of allowing refugees to leave for a price, but they promised to adopt a system called the Orderly Departure Program for people desiring to leave the country. This meant that Vietnam would clamp down on its "refugee business" and reduce the exodus by permitting only a certain number of people to depart annually. The program, which was supervised by the United Nations, worked. It allowed only several hundred departures a month, with the result that the flow out of Vietnam dwindled to just a few thousand people in the closing months of 1979.

The program remained in effect until 1986, when it was suspended by the Vietnamese due to the tense relations with the United States. By that time, it had brought nearly 50,000 people to America.[15]

Although the Orderly Departure Program stemmed the tide of those buying their way to freedom, the flood continued. Still breaking free were the multitudes from Laos and Cambodia. And coming out of Vietnam in increasing numbers were those who, deprived of the pay-for-freedom business, now escaped by stealing boats or paying smugglers to sneak them out. The flood of humanity slowly eased during the 1980s.

Despite its easing in the 1980s, the flood is still seen today. As said earlier, it continues to bring the fugitives to new lands throughout the world almost every day of the year. The United States remains the favorite destination for thousands of refugees. Because the U.S. ranks as such a favorite, a question now must be asked:

What has life been like for all the Indochinese who have become new Americans?

/ 129 /

CHAPTER

TEN

THE NEW AMERICANS

The newcomers to the United States—from the very first to the very latest—have settled in virtually all parts of the country. They are to be found in states ranging from Maine, Minnesota, Pennsylvania, and Oklahoma to Tennessee, Florida, Louisiana, and Texas. Among the states that have absorbed the greatest number are California, Illinois, New Jersey, and New York. The most popular metropolitan destinations for the new arrivals are California's Los Angeles and San Francisco Bay Area and, far across the country to the east, New York City.[1]

By far the greatest number of newcomers have settled in California. As of late 1987, the state was home to 407,800 Southeast Asians, just slightly less than half the total number in the U.S. Of the new settlers in California, some 101,000 are housed in the San Francisco Bay Area. According to the U.S. Census Bureau, close to 40,000 of the Indochinese living in the Bay Area in 1987 were Vietnamese.[2]

The story of how the newcomers have fared in the United States is one of triumphs and tribulations.

THE TRIUMPHS

Countless of the Vietnamese, Laotian, and Cambodian refugees have built successful lives for themselves in all parts of the country. They could hardly fail to do so because, right from the moment of their arrival, they showed themselves to be hardworking and ambitious. To get their new lives started, they took all types of work, some of it menial and far below the positions they had held at home. Army officers were to be found driving taxicabs. Government officials worked in laundries. One wealthy businessman swept floors and washed dishes in a restaurant.

The owner of a seafood restaurant in Mississippi will never forget the ambitious Vietnamese he once hired. In 1981, he received two shipments of oysters that needed to be shucked (needed to have their shells removed). The job was messy and hard, and the owner could find no Americans willing to take it on. And so he brought in about a dozen Vietnamese who had settled nearby. The man later said he had never met people so eager and willing to work. Added to his memory of his Vietnamese workers was his respect for their honesty. He said that he could leave tools lying about in the certainty that they would not be stolen.[3]

The new Americans, especially the Vietnamese, displayed a talent for opening businesses of their own. In 1985, *U.S. News & World Report* spoke of their success in this area. The magazine reported that countless newcomers had gone into rundown commercial districts all across the nation and had revitalized them with grocery stores, gift shops, restaurants, shopping centers, and small business offices. The magazine went on to say that, according to government figures, the newcomers—those in business for themselves and those who held salaried jobs—had earned $1.2 billion in 1982 alone and had paid approximately $15 million in taxes.[4]

Two reasons seem to account for so many successful Vietnamese businesses. First, there is the willingness of all family members to work at any type of job that will get their new lives started. Second, there is the willingness of the members to pool their earnings—sometimes among themselves and sometimes with

/ 131 /

other families—so that the funds to start a business can be quickly acquired.

Just what the willingness to work and pool their money has done for many Vietnamese is to be seen in the story of two families who settled in California. After becoming friends while traveling to Hong Kong, they remained together on arriving in the U.S. They went to work at menial jobs and then pooled whatever money was left over after their monthly expenses had been met. Today, they own a cleaning and laundry shop.[5]

Their shop earns the two families a comfortable living, but some of the success stories have come to involve millions of dollars. A 1985 issue of *Money* magazine reported on the experience of a man and his wife who fled Vietnam in 1975. A well-to-do couple, they managed to take about $15,000 in gold and jewelry with them. They settled in southern California and used their funds as a down payment on a home. Then, using the money they made when they took out a second mortgage on their home, they bought property that could be rented. They continued to buy rental property until, in 1985, they owned homes and duplexes worth $1.1 million. The man also went into the real estate business, opening an office in 1976. His earnings from the sales made by his office in 1984 totaled $75,000.[6]

While building a fine reputation as business owners, the refugees also excelled in other fields. Consider, first, the young woman who was present when President Ronald Reagan delivered his State of the Union address in 1985. An unforgettable moment in her life came when Mr. Reagan introduced her to the millions of Americans watching on television. He said that hers was a fine example of the contributions being made to the nation by the newcomers. The young woman was a West Point cadet and was

Cadet Jean Quyen Thi-Hoang Nguyen graduated from West Point in 1985, ten years after she and her family fled Vietnam.

due to be graduated in a few weeks—almost exactly ten years after she and her family had fled Vietnam.[7]

Or take the case of the young woman who grew up in a prosperous home near Saigon. When the city fell, she and her family were flown to Guam aboard a U.S. helicopter. From there, they made their way to a refugee center in Arkansas and then moved on to settle in an Italian neighborhood in Chicago. While her father and older brother worked at menial jobs, she attended the Illinois Institute of Technology on a scholarship, all the while studying to improve her English. On earning a bachelor's degree in electrical engineering, she was hired by Bell Laboratories. She went on to become a designer of computer software for Bell.[8]

A Caution

After reporting on these success stories, a caution is necessary. It would be a mistake to think that every refugee has become prosperous since arriving in the United States. The fact is that most of the success stories have been on the modest side. The newcomers still have a long way to go before catching up with the incomes earned by white families and those of other ethnic groups.

This point was made clear in a report issued by the U.S. Civil Rights Commission in 1988.[9] It revealed that the refugees are earning far less annually than all other Asian groups in the nation. The average annual income for a Vietnamese family stands at $15,859. In sharp contrast, Japanese-American families outrank all other Asian groups, bringing in an average income of $35,017 a year.

The average annual family income for non-Hispanic whites stands at $26,535, the commission reported. Korean families fall slightly below this average at $25,234. Chinese, Indian, and Filipino families rank slightly above the average.

A 1988 poll taken in the San Francisco Bay Area with its heavy Indochinese population came up with findings that supported the commission's report. It showed that more than 50 percent of the Vietnamese, Laotians, and Cambodians in the region were living on family incomes that were below the poverty line established by the U.S. The poll also showed that they were farther below the line than any other Bay Area ethnic group.[10]

THE TRIBULATIONS

It would also be a mistake to assume, after reading the various success stories, that every Indochinese refugee has received a cordial welcome in the U.S. Many of the newcomers have run into trouble as they've attempted to establish themselves.

The Americans have reacted to the strangers in their midst in various ways. In many communities, the refugees have been welcomed and have been allowed to settle without difficulty; state and federal agencies, local churches, community organizations, families, and individuals have all lent them a helping hand. In other communities, however, the reception has been anything from quietly cool to outright hostile. Much of the hostility has stemmed from the worry that the newcomers would endanger the livelihoods of the Americans living there.

This concern was dramatically evident along the nation's southern coast in the late 1970s and early 1980s.[11] There, from Florida to Texas, many Vietnamese fishermen settled in the hope of plying their trade in the Gulf of Mexico. A Mississippi fisherman, in a 1981 *National Geographic* article, spoke of what happened to his livelihood when the Vietnamese arrived. He said that he had always fished a certain stretch of water, leaving other areas to his fellow fishermen so that all would have the best chances for a good catch. But, suddenly, there were thirty to forty Vietnamese boats in the area—and then more and more. His catch fell off a third within a year. He said that he could not afford to have the Vietnamese intruding on his area. He'd been having a hard enough time earning a living before their arrival.

A Vietnamese fisherman, quoted in the same *National Geographic* article, remembered how the Mississippi fishermen had reacted with anger. Soon after he and his fellow Vietnamese entered the area, they found that the American-owned wharfs would refuse them permission to dock with their catches. Seafood buyers refused to purchase their catches. Signs appeared on the wharfs, reading "No Vietnamese Allowed." The Vietnamese fisherman claimed that the Americans fired shots at his boat and those of his friends. The tensions in one Mississippi port town became so great that the Vietnamese moved on to another area.

As bad as they were, the Mississippi troubles did not measure up to those seen in Texas. There, in the early 1980s, the competition between American and Vietnamese fishermen exploded in violence. A newcomer, harassed by an American, pulled out a gun and shot the man, killing him. When the Vietnamese went to trial, he was found innocent of murder. His act was judged to have been justifiable homicide, prompted by an unbearable harassment.

The Texas trouble eventually led to actions by the hooded Ku Klux Klan. The Klan accused the Vietnamese of being communist infiltrators and demonstrated its hatred of them by building and then burning a mock Vietnamese fishing boat.

Fortunately, although tensions are still present, the passing years have seen a gradual easing of the angers along the Gulf Coast. The newcomers seem to be gradually making a place for themselves there as they continue to fish, find jobs in restaurants, service stations, and fish processing plants, and open their own businesses. As one area resident has put it, the Vietnamese and the Americans are getting to know and be accustomed to each other.

Just as fortunately, most refugees have not met with the violence seen along the Gulf. In general, their problems have been difficulties any of us might face on settling in a land that we find strange and that finds us strange. These problems can be most readily listed and discussed by looking at a poll taken in 1988 in the San Francisco Bay Area, one of the principal destinations chosen by the refugees. It can be safely assumed that the personal problems voiced in the poll have been experienced by newcomers everywhere in the United States.

The San Francisco Bay Area Poll

Sponsored by the *San Francisco Chronicle,* the poll surveyed 200 Vietnamese adults and 200 Chinese adults on such matters as discrimination and employment problems.[12] Although the Bay Area boasts of a wide variety of Asian peoples—including Japanese, Koreans, Thais, and Malaysians—the poll was limited to the Vietnamese and Chinese because the *Chronicle* thought it would be impractical to attempt interviews with representatives of every

Asian group in the region. The newspaper also felt that the Chinese and Vietnamese would adequately reflect the views of the area's other groups.

The Vietnamese spoke of three major problem areas. They are:

The Language Barrier

The Vietnamese thought that difficulties in mastering the English language stand as a major barrier on the path to achieving financial success and winning acceptance into the society of their new country. Almost half said that their problems with the language had cost them jobs at one time or another. Nearly 54 percent claimed to have been denied job, housing, and education opportunities because of their poor English.

Mastery of English has proven especially difficult for the older people, long accustomed as they are to the language of their homeland. One older woman arrived in the Bay Area from Saigon in 1981. She was a clerk-typist at home, but said that she had been unable to find work because of her continuing poor English. Children, on the other hand, appear to have had little trouble in learning English, in part because they attend public schools, watch television, and make friends with English-speaking youngsters.

Discrimination

About 60 percent of the Vietnamese told the pollsters that they have come up against racial discrimination during their U.S. years. They've put up with examples of prejudice that range from slight slurs to such serious matters as housing discrimination. Twenty-one percent of the interviewees believed they had been denied opportunities in housing, education, and employment because of their ethnic background.

Many of the discriminatory acts have hurt deeply. Their children, some of the Vietnamese said, have complained of being called "Slanty Eyes" and "Yellow" by their classmates or of being the source of derision because of their speech patterns and accents. One woman who escaped Saigon in 1975 now lives in a housing project inhabited mainly by blacks and Hispanics. She told the poll that many of her neighbors are suspicious of her and that some simply don't like her because they find her "different." Area children have thrown eggs at her house so often that she has given up trying to clear away the mess.

Several Vietnamese recalled that they were the dominant racial and cultural group back in their homeland. They admitted to finding the discrimination particularly hard to handle because they are new to the experience of being members of a minority group.

Understanding a New Land

Most of the Vietnamese said that they would like to keep something of their homeland's culture while at the same time becoming sufficiently "Americanized" to feel a part of their new country. But they are having trouble understanding the U.S. society and establishing a place for themselves in it.

Many find the customs and the ways of life here strange. As a result, they tend to stay away from such American events as baseball and football games. Likewise, they tend to avoid making friends with the Americans around them. (Other studies of the Vietnamese in America and remarks by officials who work with the refugees have left little doubt that these tendencies are causing resentment among the Americans and are adding to the discrimination felt by the newcomers. The newcomers are seen by many Americans as cliquish, distant, and unfriendly.)

The poll also revealed the Vietnamese fear that their children, in learning English, watching television, and befriending their schoolmates, will become so Americanized that they will forget the traditions of their homeland, among them a deep respect for family ties. When speaking of their children, some of the Vietnamese expressed the feeling that they are "changing places" with the youngsters. Because the children are learning English and are growing increasingly comfortable with U.S. life, they are assuming leadership roles in such family activities as shopping and dealing with strangers. The parents said that they themselves are becoming the children of the family, while the children are becoming the parents.

Despite these problems, the Bay Area Vietnamese look to the future with great hope. When asked if they believed their ethnic group would be better off twenty years from now, almost all—92 percent—answered in the affirmative. Six percent felt that their situation would still be much as it is today. A mere 2 percent prophesied that their status would be worse.

Much of the Vietnamese hope for an improved future is based on a faith that their children will succeed. Toward this end, the children are urged to study hard and excel in their schoolwork so that they may go on to the university work that will lead to better jobs.

THE FLIGHT TO FREEDOM TODAY

As was said earlier, the influx of Indochinese is continuing today. But the rate of entry in recent times has been lower than during the late 1970s and early 1980s. You'll recall from Chapter Nine that the Orderly Departure Program adopted by Vietnam during the 1979 United Nations conference on the refugee problem was in great part responsible for the reduction. It put an end to the Vietnamese business of freedom for a price and saw Vietnam permit several hundred people to leave the country monthly. The program remained in effect until 1986, when it was suspended by Hanoi because of tense relations with the U.S. By that time, approximately 50,000 people had moved to the United States under the program.

Still, a few people were allowed to leave Vietnam during the subsequent months. Then, in 1988, negotiations between the United States and Vietnam brought a new development in the refugee situation and promised a sudden increase in the flow of newcomers to American shores. Vietnam agreed to allow some 50,000 citizens to depart the country over what was expected to be a two-year period. Among them were to be 11,000 people who had been imprisoned by the Hanoi government because they had supported South Vietnam during the war. Also to be given permission to leave were the unfortunate young people known as Amerasians.

The Amerasian Children

Amerasians are the children born of American servicemen and Vietnamese women during the war.[13] Their number is unknown

/ 139 /

but has been estimated at anywhere from 8,000 to 15,000. Whatever the true figure might be, the young people, most of whom are now in their late teens, are considered to be among the world's most unfortunate humans.

Shunned and scorned by the Vietnamese population because of their American blood, they are poorly educated and lack the training for any sort of skilled labor. One seventeen-year-old who is now in America has expressed her joy at not having to sew shirts in a clothing factory for 3 cents each. Some, on the deaths of their mothers, have been left to fend for themselves on the streets, with even their relatives unwilling to take them in. So far as the Hanoi government is concerned, the street children do not officially exist; they have eked out bare livings selling cigarettes on street corners, stealing, and doing whatever odd jobs have come their way. To the Vietnamese, the Amerasians have long been known as *bui doi*— the "dust of life."

Two thousand youngsters were permitted to come to the United States under the Orderly Departure Program. Many of the new arrivals could barely read and write. Many were in poor health, with malnutrition being common. Almost all were in need of dental attention. And almost all, after years of scorn and hardship, had disturbingly low opinions of themselves and their possibilities for a happy future.

Many servicemen had planned to marry their Vietnamese sweethearts but had been separated from them when shipped home at war's end. Consequently, a number of men, feeling a deep sense of responsibility, have attempted to locate the Vietnamese mothers and children over the years. Most have met with failure because of the absence of diplomatic ties between the United States and Vietnam; such ties would have enabled the establishment of agencies to facilitate the efforts. Several men, however, have traveled to Vietnam on learning the whereabouts of their orphaned youngsters and have managed to bring them home. Others, on hearing that their children were coming to the U.S., have been on hand to greet them and take them into their homes, even though the men were now married to American women and had families. Sadly, most of the fathers have shown an unwillingness to find or be reunited with

Poor people of Saigon retrieve scrap iron
from a garbage heap to sell on the open market.
The girl on the right is an Amerasian.

their children, not wanting to have a strange newcomer upset the lives they have built for themselves since the war.

Presently waiting to come to the United States is a combined total of 20,000 to 30,000 Amerasians and their relatives. Prior to the 1988 U.S.-Vietnamese agreement, the children were arriving in the United States at the rate of 200 to 300 a month. Under the agreement, their number is expected to vault to more than 1,000 a month. Some will be reunited with their fathers. Most will be housed in foster homes, with American and Vietnamese families.

Much of the work of resettling the youngsters and the relatives who accompany them will be done by volunteer agencies, a chief one being the Amerasian Resettlement Planning Committee. The committee says that the children will require special care if they are to launch successful lives in the United States, this because they have suffered such scorn and mistreatment throughout their young years.

To help matters along, Vietnam and the United States announced in late 1988 plans to open a center in Hanoi for Amerasian children. The center will help orphaned youngsters and those who are seeking to emigrate to the U.S.[14]

It can only be hoped that, with affection and guidance, these young people will find in the United States a long overdue contentment and success and that, in common with countless refugees who fled Indochina in search of a new life, they will be able to make a contribution to the social, economic, and cultural richness of the United States. It will be then that we can look on the fifth legacy of the Vietnam War as having been a happy one.

NOTES

INTRODUCTION

1. J. Gardner, "Answers at Last?" *The Nation*, 11 April 1987, 460.

CHAPTER ONE
THE HATED WAR

1. "We're Still Prisoners of War," *Newsweek*, 15 April 1985, 37; L. Morrow, "A Bloody Rite of Passage," *Time*, 15 April 1985, 22.
2. The material on the roots of the Vietnam War and the history of the war, its effects on the American people, and its outcome is developed from: E. Doyle, S. Lippsman, and the Editors of Boston Publishing Company, *The Vietnam Experience: America Takes Over, 1965–67* (Boston: Boston Publishing, 1982), 141; C. Dougan, S. Weiss, and the Editors of Boston Publishing Company, *The Vietnam Experience: Nineteen Sixty-Eight* (Boston: Boston Publishing, 1983), 10–12, 82–83; F. Fitzgerald, *Fire in the Lake: The Vietnamese and the Americans in Vietnam* (Boston: Little, Brown, 1972), 66–67, 80, 85, 149, 303, 404–408; A. Isaacs, *Without Honor* (Baltimore: Johns Hopkins University Press, 1983), 61; J. T. McAlister, Jr., *Viet Nam: The Origins of Revolution* (New York: Alfred A. Knopf, 1969), 351–365; D. Lawson, *The United States in the Vietnam War* (New York: Thomas Y. Crowell, 1981), 14–15, 17–20, 111–113; E. F. Dolan, Jr., *Amnesty: The American Puzzle* (New York: Franklin Watts, 1976), 16–24.

CHAPTER TWO
WELCOME TO ALIENATION

1. The material on the differences between the welcome home given the Vietnam veterans and those of the century's three earlier wars is developed from: E. Doyle, T. Maitland, and the Editors of Boston Publishing Company, *The Vietnam Experience: The Aftermath, 1975–85* (Boston: Boston Publishing, 1985), 126.
2. The material on the unhappy welcome home given many Vietnam veterans is developed from: *The Aftermath*, 126, 128; L. Morrow, "A Bloody Rite of Passage," *Time*, 15 April 1985, 23; and interviews with seven Vietnam veterans.
3. The material on the attitudes of the American public toward the Vietnam veteran and the contributions made to them by the entertainment media is developed from: *The Aftermath*, 128, 131; Morrow, 24; E. F. Dolan, Jr., *Hollywood Goes to War* (Greenwich, Ct.: Bison Books, 1985), 120–122.
4. The material on the successful lives that the majority of the Vietnam veterans made for themselves is developed from: "Fresh Light on a Group Portrait," *U.S. News & World Report*, 23 May 1988, 12; L. Roberts, "Vietnam's Psychological Toll," *Science*, 8 July 1988, 161; S. Powell, "The Healing Nation," from "Vietnam: The Lasting Impact," *U.S. News & World Report*, 22 April 1985, 37; Morrow, 24; *The Aftermath*, 128.
5. *The Aftermath*, 142.
6. E. F. Dolan, *MIA: Missing in Action* (New York: Franklin Watts, 1989), 26; *The Aftermath*, 142.
7. *The Aftermath*, 125–126.
8. The material on the Vietnam Veterans Memorial is developed from: Morrow, 25; "The Healing Nation," 36; *The Aftermath*, 142–146.
9. "Woman Viet Vet Statue Gets an OK," *San Francisco Chronicle*, 12 May 1988; "Memorial for Women Vets of Viet War," *San Francisco Chronicle*, 22 October 1988.

CHAPTER THREE
INVISIBLE WOUNDS

1. The statistics on drug and alcohol abuse among the troops in Vietnam is developed from: E. Doyle, T. Maitland, and the Editors of Boston Publishing Company, *The Vietnam Experience: The Aftermath, 1975–85* (Boston: Boston Publishing, 1982), 128, 131.
2. The material on the psychological problems suffered by many veterans is developed from: S. Powell, "The Healing Nation," from "Vietnam: The Lasting Impact," *U.S. News & World Report*, 22 April 1985, 36; L. Roberts, "Vietnam's Psychological Toll," *Science*, 8 July 1988, 160–161; *The Aftermath*, 132, 137; *The National Vietnam Veterans Readjustment Study*, as submitted to the U.S. Senate Committee on Veterans' Affairs, July 14, 1988, 21–22.

/ 144 /

3. The material on veterans in trouble with the law is developed from: *The Aftermath,* 131–132.
4. The material on the reasons for drug, alcohol, psychological, and criminal problems suffered by many veterans is developed from: *The Aftermath,* 131; Roberts, 161; interviews with a World War II veteran and a Vietnam veteran.

CHAPTER FOUR
HOW WELL HAVE THE
VETERANS FARED?

1. The material on the Vietnam Experience Study is developed from: "Veterans Have More Stress Complaints Than Other GIs," *San Francisco Chronicle,* 12 May 1988; "Fresh Light on a Group Portrait," *U.S. News & World Report,* 23 July 1988, 12; *Science,* 8 July 1988, 159–161.

CHAPTER FIVE
THE MYSTERY OF AGENT ORANGE

1. The material on Operation Ranch Hand, its purposes, and its extent is developed from: W. Lowther, "A Bittersweet Victory," *Maclean's,* 21 May 1984, 52; J. V. Lamar, Jr., "Winning Peace with Honor: A Truce Is Negotiated in the Battle of Agent Orange," *Time,* 21 May 1984, 39; N. Zamichow, "Vietnam Workers Stonewalled on Agent Orange Dangers," *Ms.,* August 1986, 26; J. Gardner, "Answers at Last?" *The Nation,* 11 April 1987, 460; E. Zumwalt III, as told to J. Grossman, "A War with Hope," *Health,* June 1987, 88.
2. The material on the illnesses that were seen after exposure to Agent Orange is developed from: R. Shaplen, *Bitter Victory* (New York: Harper & Row, 1986), 34–35; "Vietnam Vets, Chemical Cos. Settle Agent Orange Suit," *Facts on File,* 11 May 1984, 336; Lamar, 39; Lowther, 52.
3. Lamar, 34.
4. The material on the chemical components in Agent Orange, its dioxin content, and the known dangers of dioxin to animals is developed from: J. L. Fox, "Agent Orange Study Is Like a Chameleon," *Science,* 16 March 1984, 1156; Gardner, 460; Lowther, 52.
5. The material on chloracne and soft tissue sarcoma is developed from: Fox, 1157; Lamar, 39; Lowther, 52.
6. Lamar, 39.
7. The material on Elmo Zumwalt III is developed from: Grossman, 86, 88; E. R. Zumwalt, Jr., and E. Zumwalt III, "Agent Orange and the Anguish of an American Family," *New York Times Magazine,* 24 August 1986, 32–34; "Milestones," *Time,* 22 August 1988, 69.
8. The material on Kammy McCleery Malloy and other women workers in Vietnam is developed from: Zamichow, 26.

/ 145 /

CHAPTER SIX
MEDICAL AND LEGAL ACTIONS

1. The material on the study of the Ranch Hand personnel is developed from: J. L. Fox, "Agent Orange Study Is Like a Chameleon," *Science,* 16 March 1984, 1156–1157.
2. The material on the CDC study of the Atlanta children is developed from: J. Raloff, "Agent Orange and Birth Defects Risk," *Science News,* 25 August 1984, 117; "Agent Orange: No Link to Birth Defects?" *Newsweek,* 27 August 1984, 24; "Study Doubts Birth Defects Link," *Facts on File,* 31 August 1984, 640–641.
3. The material on the Australian study is developed from: Constance Holden, "VA to Study Twins," *Science,* 16 March 1984, 1157; "Agent Orange Rejected in Health Claims," *Facts on File,* 20 September 1984, 699.
4. The material on the criticisms of the Agent Orange studies is developed from: Fox, 1157; Raloff, 117; "Agent Orange: No Link to Birth Defects," 24; "Study Doubts Birth Defects Link," 641; "Agent Orange Rejected in Health Claims," 699; J. Gardner, "Answers at Last?" *The Nation,* 11 April 1987, 461.
5. Gardner, 462.
6. The material on the Agent Orange studies being conducted by the states is developed from: Gardner, 461–462.
7. J. V. Lamar, Jr., "Winning Peace with Honor: A Truce Is Negotiated in the Battle of Agent Orange," *Time,* 21 May 1984, 39.
8. The material on the Agent Orange class action lawsuit is developed from W. Lowther, "A Bittersweet Victory," *Maclean's,* 21 May 1984, 52; Aric Press with A. McDaniel and B. Burgower, "A Fast Deal on Agent Orange," *Newsweek,* 21 May 1984, 56; Lamar, 39–40; "Agent Orange Payout Planned," *Facts on File,* 20 June 1985, 482; P. Dwyer, "The Agent Orange Settlement Still Unsettled," *Business Week,* 15 September 1985, 47; "Agent Orange Settlement Affirmed," *Facts on File,* 1 May 1987, 313; "Payments for Agent Orange Victims," *San Francisco Chronicle,* 6 July 1988.

CHAPTER SEVEN
MISSING IN ACTION

1. T. A. Boettcher and J. A. Rehyansky, "We Can Keep You . . . Forever," *National Review,* 21 August 1981, 958; A. Isaacs, *Without Honor* (Baltimore: Johns Hopkins University Press, 1983), 61.
2. A. Deming, "The Hunt for the Lost MIA's," *Newsweek,* 2 December 1985, 60.
3. "Tracking the Last MIA's," *Newsweek,* 4 March 1985, 37.
4. "Missing," *Life,* November 1987, 113.
5. Deming, 60.
6. J. Rosenthal, "The Myth of the Lost POWs," *New Republic,* 1 July 1985, 17.

7. Isaacs, 65.
8. The material on the work and problems of the joint military team is developed from: Isaacs, 64–68, 134–135.
9. The material on the suspected Vietnamese "economic blackmail" is developed from: G. Kolko, *Anatomy of a War* (New York: Pantheon, 1985), 611; Isaacs, 131–134.
10. Isaacs, 137.
11. The material on the House Select Committee on Missing Persons in Southeast Asia, its work, and the criticism it generated is developed from: Rehyansky, 961; Rosenthal, 18.
12. Information provided by the National League of Families of American Prisoners and Missing in Southeast Asia.
13. The material on the objections to the House Select Committee's report from within the committee is developed from: "Why—Mr. President?" a radio address by Lt. Col. (ret.) S. W. Jones, prepared for broadcast on Boston radio station WHET in September 1977.
14. The material on the Woodcock Commission is developed from: P. A. Gigot, "Lost or Merely Forgotten?" *National Review*, 17 August 1979, 1036–1037; Rehyansky, 959.
15. Rosenthal, 18.
16. "Missing," 114.
17. "Daring Mission, Dashed Hopes," *Time*, 1 June 1981, 31; R. L. Berke, "POWs Alive in Vietnam, Report Concludes," *New York Times*, 30 September 1986; R. Shaplen, *Bitter Victory* (New York: Harper & Row, 1986), 62; Rosenthal, 15.
18. The material on Robert Garwood is developed from: B. Poos, "POWs: Pawns of War," *Vietnam*, a publication of *Soldier of Fortune*, February 1986, 83–84; B. Paul, "POWs: The Evidence Is There; Now Let's Act," *Wall Street Journal*, 21 April 1986.

CHAPTER EIGHT
THE QUEST FOR THE MISSING

1. The figures for the reported sightings of living MIAs in Indochina are derived from: M. Beck, M. Lord, and R. LaBrecque, "Exploiting the MIA Families," *Newsweek*, 11 April 1983, 34; J. Rosenthal, "The Myth of the Lost POWs," *New Republic*, 1 July 1985, 15; "Missing," *Life*, November 1987, 114; S. Erlanger, "Missing in Action: From a Lost War, a Haunting Echo That Won't Be Stilled," *New York Times*, 31 August 1988.
2. "Daring Mission, Dashed Hopes," *Time*, 1 June 1981, 31; "A Secret Mission to Search for MIAs," *Newsweek*, 1 June 1981, 54.
3. B. Paul, "POWs Won't Be Found Without Cost," *Wall Street Journal*, 24 April 1985.
4. P. Gigot, "Lost or Merely Forgotten?" *National Review*, 17 August 1979, 1038; "Missing," 116; Paul.

5. The material on the work of the Defense Intelligence Agency is developed from: T. D. Boettcher and J. A. Rehyansky, "We Can Keep You . . . Forever," *National Review,* 21 August 1981, 961; "Missing," 116; Beck et al., 34; Rosenthal, 15; Paul.

6. The material on the criticisms leveled against the DIA is developed from: Paul.

7. "The Search for Missing Servicemen," *Newsweek,* 10 November 1980, 16–17; Gigot, 961.

8. A. Isaacs, *Without Honor* (Baltimore: Johns Hopkins University Press, 1983), 132.

9. Gigot, 962.

10. J. L. Pate, "Missing in Action," *Soldier of Fortune,* July 1968, 33; information provided by the National League of Families of American Prisoners and Missing in Southeast Asia.

11. The material on the connection between the number of returned MIA remains and U.S.-Vietnamese relations is developed from information provided by the National League of Families.

12. Beck et al., 34; information provided by the National League of Families.

13. R. T. Zintl, "Jungle Hunt for Missing Airmen," *Time,* 25 February 1985, 21; J. Willwerth, "Excavating the Recent Past," *Time,* 4 March 1985, 49; "Tracking the Last MIA's," *Newsweek,* 4 March 1985, 37; Pate, 32.

14. P. T. White, "Missing in Action," *National Geographic,* November 1986, 692–696; information provided by the National League of Families.

15. A. Deming, "MIA's: A Surprise from Hanoi," *Newsweek,* 22 July 1985, 34; "Vietnam to U.S.—26 More Coffins," *U.S. News & World Report,* 26 August 1985, 9.

16. "Vietnam: The Hunt for MIA's," *Newsweek,* 2 December 1985, 60.

17. Zintl, 21.

18. The material on Vietnam's economy is developed from: "The Lost Americans," *Newsweek,* 20 January 1986, 27; "Inside Vietnam: What a Former POW Found," *U.S. News & World Report,* 11 March 1985, 33; Deming, 34.

19. The material on the events in Cambodia is developed from: F. Ponchaud, *Cambodia: Year Zero* (New York: Holt, Rinehart and Winston, 1977), 1–2, 52–71, 82–83; S. Karnow, *Vietnam: A History* (New York: Viking Press, 1983), 685–686; Isaacs, 285–289; "Cambodians in Retreat," *Facts on File,* 1–5 January 1979, 1; "U.S. Arms Arrive in Thailand," *Facts on File,* 11 July 1980, 508.

20. The material on Vietnam's intention to withdraw from Cambodia and the plan for the joint U.S.-Vietnamese search for MIAs is developed from: "U.S., Vietnam Set to Hunt MIAs Together" (reprinted from *Los Angeles Times*), *San Francisco Chronicle,* 22 July 1988; "Vietnam Pulls Out of MIA Search" (reprinted from *Washington Post*), *San Francisco Chronicle,* 4 August 1988; "Hanoi to Aid on Searches," *New York Times,* 31 August 1988.

21. "U.S.-Laos Agreement on MIA Searches," *San Francisco Chronicle,* January 5, 1989.

CHAPTER NINE
FLIGHT TO A NEW LIFE

1. The figures on the worldwide resettlement of the refugees and those on the resettlement of the refugees in the United States, Canada, Australia, and France are dervied from: "U.S. Not Interested in Talks on Refugees," *San Francisco Chronicle*, 8 July 1988.
2. R. Waters, "The Ones Who Went Home," *San Francisco Examiner*, 28 August 1988.
3. S. Powell, "The Healing Nation," from "Vietnam: The Lasting Impact," *U.S. News & World Report*, 22 April 1985, 36.
4. The material on the flight from Vietnam that began as Saigon was falling is developed from: E. Doyle, T. Maitland, and the Editors of Boston Publishing Company, *The Vietnam Experience: The Aftermath, 1975–85* (Boston: Boston Publishing, 1985), 26–30; D. Lawson, *The United States in the Vietnam War* (New York: Thomas Y. Crowell, 1981), 131–133.
5. *The Aftermath*, 43.
6. The material on the South Vietnamese army captain is developed from an interview with the captain, who preferred not to be identified.
7. The material on the business of freeing refugees for a price and the business of manufacturing false identity papers is developed from: *The Aftermath*, 37.
8. The material on the Vietnamese family that posed as a Chinese family is developed from: "The Boat People," from a special report on the Vietnam War and its aftermath, *Maclean's*, 29 April 1985, 46.
9. The material on the Thai pirates is developed from: H. Arden, "Troubled Odyssey of Vietnamese Fishermen," *National Geographic*, September 1981, 386; *The Aftermath*, 32, 34; and from an interview with a former boat person.
10. *The Aftermath*, 32, 34.
11. Ibid., 32, 34.
12. Ibid., 40; interview with a former boat person.
13. Ibid., 43.
14. Ibid., 43.
15. E. Fernandez, "Amerasian Children Coming Home," *San Francisco Examiner*, 11 October 1987.

CHAPTER TEN
THE NEW AMERICANS

1. "Immigration Expected to Reach Historic Highs in '80s," (from *Washington Post*), *San Francisco Chronicle*, 25 July 1988.
2. R. G. McLeod, "Southeast Asians Head West," *San Francisco Chronicle*, 19 July 1988.
3. H. Arden, "Troubled Odyssey of Vietnamese Fishermen," *National Geographic*, September 1981, 385.

4. S. Powell, "The Healing Nation," from "Vietnam: The Lasting Impact," *U.S. News & World Report,* 22 April 1985, 36.
5. Developed from an interview with the two Vietnamese families.
6. L. Lawrence, "Four Vietnamese Success Stories," *Money,* March 1985, 45–46.
7. Powell, 36.
8. Lawrence, 41.
9. The material on the Civil Rights Commission report is developed from: "Asian American Family Income Is Higher" (from *Washington Post*), *San Francisco Chronicle,* 16 July 1988.
10. L. A. Chung and M. McCabe, "Bay Area Asians Counting on Economic Success, Poll Says," *San Francisco Chronicle,* 16 July 1988.
11. The material on the American-Vietnamese problems along the Mississippi and Texas coasts is developed from: *National Geographic,* September 1981, 386–387, 390, 394.
12. The material on the San Francisco Bay Area poll is developed from: L. A. Chung and M. McCabe, "Facing the Hopes and Fears of Assimilation," *San Francisco Chronicle,* 25 July 1988; *San Francisco Chronicle,* 26 July 1988.
13. The material on the Amerasian children is developed from: M. Beck, F. Gibney, Jr., S. Doherty, H. Morris, M. Liu, M. Reese, and M. Anderson, "Where Is My Father?" from "The Legacy of Vietnam," *Newsweek,* 15 April 1985, 54–57; E. Fernandez, "Amerasian Children Coming Home," *San Francisco Examiner,* 11 October 1987; N. Cooper and R. Moreau, "Go Back to Your Country," *Newsweek,* 14 March 1988, 34–35; T. Bizjak, "4 Americans' Chancy Quest for Their Kids," *San Francisco Chronicle,* 20 June 1988; T. Bizjak, "Amerasian Youth Due 'Home' Tonight," *San Francisco Chronicle,* 1 July 1988; T. Bizjak, "Dream Come True for Amerasian Boy and His Dad," *San Francisco Chronicle,* 2 July 1988; K. Teltsch, "Amerasian Influx Expected by U.S.," *New York Times,* 9 October 1988.
14. "Vietnam Center for GI's Kids," *San Francisco Chronicle,* December 2, 1988.

BIBLIOGRAPHY

BOOKS

Bloodworth, Dennis. *An Eye for the Dragon: Southeast Asia Observed, 1954–1970.* New York: Farrar, Straus and Giroux, 1970.

Dolan, Edward F., Jr. *Amnesty: The American Puzzle.* New York: Franklin Watts, 1976.

_____. *Hollywood Goes to War.* Greenwich, Ct.: Bison Books, 1985.

_____. *MIA: Missing in Action.* New York: Franklin Watts, 1989.

Doyle, Edward, Terrence Maitland, and the Editors of Boston Publishing Company. *The Vietnam Experience: The Aftermath.* Boston: Boston Publishing, 1985.

Doyle, Edward, Samuel Lippsman, and the Editors of Boston Publishing Company. *The Vietnam Experience: America Takes Over 1965–67.* Boston: Boston Publishing, 1982.

Edelman, Bernard, ed., for the New York Veterans Memorial Commission. *Dear America: Letters Home from Vietnam.* New York: W. W. Norton, 1985.

Fincher, E. B. *The Vietnam War.* New York: Franklin Watts, 1980.

Fitzgerald, Frances. *Fire in the Lake: The Vietnamese and the Americans in Vietnam.* Boston: Little, Brown, 1972.

Isaacs, Arnold R. *Without Honor: Defeat in Vietnam and Cambodia.* Baltimore: Johns Hopkins University Press, 1983.

Karnow, Stanley. *Vietnam: A History.* New York: Viking Press, 1983.

Kolko, Gabriel. *Anatomy of a War: Vietnam, the United States, and the Modern Historical Experience.* New York: Pantheon Books, 1985.

Lawson, Don. *The War in Vietnam.* New York: Franklin Watts, 1981.

_____. *The United States in the Vietnam War.* New York: Crowell, 1981.

Liston, Robert J. *Home from the War.* New York: Simon & Schuster, 1973.

Mabie, Margaret C. J. *Vietnam: There and Here.* New York: Holt, Rinehart and Winston, 1985.

McAlister, John T., Jr. *Viet Nam: The Origins of Revolution.* New York: Alfred A. Knopf, 1969.

Ponchaud, Francois. *Cambodia: Year Zero.* New York: Holt, Rinehart and Winston, 1977.

Salisbury, Harrison, ed. *Vietnam Reconstructed: Lessons from a War.* New York: Harper & Row, 1984.

Santoli, Al. *To Bear Any Burden: The Vietnam War and Its Aftermath in the Words of Americans and Southeast Asians.* New York: E. P. Dutton, 1985.

Scholl-Latour, Robert. *Death in the Rice Fields: An Eyewitness Account of Vietnam's Three Wars, 1945–1970.* New York: St. Martin's Press, 1979.

Shaplen, Robert. *The Road From War: Vietnam 1965–1970.* New York: Harper & Row, 1970.

_____. *Bitter Victory.* New York: Harper & Row, 1986.

Trager, Frank N. *Why Vietnam?* New York: Frederick A. Praeger, 1966.

Weiss, Stephen, Clark Dougan, David Fulghum, Denis Kennedy, and the Editors of Boston Publishing Company. *The Vietnam Experience: A War Remembered.* Boston: Boston Publishing, 1986.

MAGAZINE ARTICLES

"Agent Orange: No Link to Birth Defects?" *Newsweek,* 27 August 1984.

Andersen, Kurt. "A Pinched and Hermetic Land," from a special report on the Vietnam War. *Time,* 15 April 1985.

_____. "Hush, Timmy—This Is Like a Church," from a special report on the Vietnam War. *Time,* 15 April 1985.

Arden, Harvey. "Troubled Odyssey of Vietnamese Fishermen." *National Geographic,* September 1981.

Beck, Melinda. "Exploiting the MIA Families." *Newsweek,* 11 April 1983.

Beck, Melinda, Frank Gibney, Jr., Shawn Doherty, Holly Morris, Melinda Liu, Michael Reese and Monroe Anderson. "Where Is My Father?" from "The Legacy of Vietnam." *Newsweek,* 15 April 1985.

Boettcher, Thomas D., and Joseph A. Rehyansky. "We Can Keep You . . . Forever." *National Review,* 21 August 1981.

Church, George J. "Lessons from a Lost War," from a special report on the Vietnam War. *Time,* 15 April 1985.

Clifton, Tony, and Ron Moreau. "A Wounded Land," from "The Legacy of Vietnam." *Newsweek,* 15 April 1985.

Cooper, Nancy, and Ron Moreau. "Go Back to Your Country." *Newsweek,* 14 March 1988.

Deming, Angus. "MIA's: A Surprise from Hanoi." *Newsweek,* 22 July 1985.

————. "The Rambo Syndrome: Are Some MIAs Still POWs?" *Newsweek,* 20 January 1986.

————. "Vietnam: The Hunt for MIA's." *Newsweek,* 2 December 1985.

Dudney, Robert S. "Armed Forces: Proud and Prepared," from "Vietnam: The Lasting Impact." *U.S. News & World Report,* 22 April 1985.

————. "U.S. in the World: A Stronger Hand," from "Vietnam: The Lasting Impact." *U.S. News & World Report,* 22 April 1985.

Dwyer, Paula. "The Agent Orange Settlement Still Unsettled." *Business Week,* 15 September 1985.

Fineman, Howard. "Laos: A Secret Mission to Search for MIA's." *Newsweek,* 1 June 1981.

Fox, Jeffrey L. "Agent Orange Study Is Like a Chameleon." *Science,* 16 March 1984.

"Fresh Light on a Group Portrait." *U.S. News & World Report,* 23 May 1988.

Gardner, Janet. "Answers at Last?" *The Nation,* 11 April 1987.

Gee, Marcus. "A Crippled Nation," from a special report on the Vietnam War. *Maclean's,* 29 April 1985.

Getlin, Josh. "Hearts and Bones." *Los Angeles Times Magazine,* 12 October 1986.

Gigot, Paul A. "Lost or Merely Forgotten?" *National Review,* 17 August 1979.

Gray, Malcolm. "Saigon's Final Days," from a special report on the Vietnam War. *Maclean's,* 15 April 1985.

Greenberg, Nikki Finke. "Starting Over," from "The Legacy of Vietnam." *Newsweek,* 15 April 1985.

Greenfield, Meg. "Vietnam: Lessons Still Unlearned." *Newsweek,* 25 February 1985.

"Hearts and Minds," from "The Legacy of Vietnam." *Newsweek,* 15 April 1985.

Henry, William A. "Daring Mission, Dashed Hopes." *Time,* 1 June 1981.

Hitchens, Christopher. "Minority Report." *The Nation,* 14 June 1986.

"Inside Vietnam: What a Former POW Found." *U.S. News & World Report,* 11 March 1985.

Iyer, Pico. "Colonel Gritz's Dubious Mission." *Time,* 4 April 1983.

Kaylor, Robert, with Walter A. Taylor. "Dominoes That Did Not Fall," from "Vietnam: The Lasting Impact." *U.S. News & World Report,* 22 April 1985.

Lamar, Jacob V., Jr. "Winning Peace with Honor: A Truce Is Negotiated in the Battle of Agent Orange." *Time,* 21 May 1984.

"The Lost Americans." *Newsweek,* 20 January 1986.

Laurence, Leslie. "Four Vietnamese Success Stories." *Money,* March 1985.

Lowther, William. "A Bittersweet Victory." *Maclean's,* 21 May 1984.

Merick, Wendell S. " 'It Didn't Have to End This Way,' " from "Vietnam: The Lasting Impact." *U.S. News & World Report,* 15 April 1985.

Miller, Robert, with Bill Gladstone, Doug Clarke, Terry Hargreaves, Bruce Wallace, and Ian Austen. "And the Memory Lives," from a special report on the Vietnam War. *Maclean's,* 29 April 1985.

"Missing." *Life,* November 1987.

Morganthau, Tom, with Kim Willsenson, John Walcott, Nicholas M. Horrock, and Gerald C. Lubenow. "We're Still Prisoners of War, from "The Legacy of Vietnam." *Newsweek,* 15 April 1985.

Morrow, Lance. "A Bloody Rite of Passage." *Time,* 15 April 1985.

Pate, James L. "Missing in Action." *Soldier of Fortune,* July 1986.

Poos, Bob. "POW/MIAs: Pawns of War." *Vietnam,* a publication of *Soldier of Fortune,* February 1986.

Powell, Stewart. "The Healing Nation," from "Vietnam: The Lasting Impact." *U.S. News & World Report,* 22 April 1985.

"POW's in Vietnam: Fact or Fiction?" *U.S. News & World Report,* 28 October 1985.

Press, Arik, with Ann McDaniel and Barbara Burgower. "A Fast Deal on Agent Orange." *Newsweek,* 21 May 1984.

Raloff, J. "Agent Orange and Birth Defects Risk." *Science News,* 25 August 1984.

Roberts, Leslie. "Vietnam's Psychological Toll." *Science,* 8 July 1988.

Rosenthal, James. "The Myth of the Lost POWs." *New Republic,* 1 July 1985.

"The Search for Missing Servicemen." *Newsweek,* 10 November 1980.

"Still Missing: The Search for Vietnam's War Dead Takes Puzzling New Turns." *Life,* July 1986.

Strasser, Steven, with Martin Kasindorf, Richard Manning, and Vern E. Smith. "55 Days of Shame," from "The Legacy of Vietnam." *Newsweek,* 15 April 1985.

"Tracking the Last MIA's." *Newsweek,* 4 March 1985.

"VA to Study Twins." *Science,* 16 March 1984.

"Vietnam to U.S.—26 More Coffins." *U.S. News & World Report,* 26 August 1985.

Wallace, Bruce, Paul Berton, Robert Block, Douglas Clark, and Diane Lucknow. "The Boat People," from a special report on the Vietnam War. *Maclean's,* 29 April 1985.

Watson, Russell. "The Lessons of Vietnam." *Newsweek,* 16 May 1988.

Whitaker, Mary. "The Lost Americans." *Newsweek,* 20 January 1986.

White, Peter T. "Missing in Action." *National Geographic,* November 1986.

Willwerth, James. "Excavating the Recent Past." *Time,* 4 March 1985.

Zamichow, Nora. "Vietnam Workers Stonewalled on Agent Orange Dangers." *Ms.,* August 1986.

Zintl, Robert T. "Jungle Hunt for Missing Airmen." *Time,* 25 February 1985.

Zumwalt, Elmo, III, as told to John Grossman. "A War with Hope." *Health,* June 1987.

Zumwalt, Elmo, III, and Elmo R. Zumwalt, Jr. "Agent Orange and the Anguish of an American Family." *New York Times Magazine,* 24 August 1986.

NEWSPAPER ARTICLES

"Agent Orange Rejected in Health Claims." *Facts on File,* 20 September 1984.

"Agent Orange Settlement Affirmed." *Facts on File,* 1 May 1987.

"Agent Orange Victims Compensated." *San Francisco Chronicle,* 29 July 1988.

"Asian American Income Is Higher." *San Francisco Chronicle* (from *Washington Post*), 16 July 1988.

"Asian Americans Talk About Prejudice." *San Francisco Chronicle,* 25 July 1988.

"Asians Optimistic About Their Future." *San Francisco Chronicle,* 26 July 1988.

"Asia Supplies the World with Workers." *San Francisco Chronicle* (from *The Economist*), 21 September 1988.

Baer, Susan. "A Convention and the Lessons of Chaos," *San Francisco Chronicle* (from *Baltimore Sun*), 20 July 1988.

Berke, Richard L. "P.O.W.'s Alive in Vietnam, Report Concludes." *New York Times,* 30 September 1986.

Bizjak, Tony. "4 Americans' Chancy Quest for Their Kids." *San Francisco Chronicle,* 20 June 1988.

————. "Meeting the Kids They Left Behind." *San Francisco Chronicle,* 21 June 1988.

————. "Parents, Children Working to Break Down Barriers." *San Francisco Chronicle,* 24 June 1988.

————. "Parents Given 1 Child, Promises." *San Francisco Chronicle,* 27 June 1988.

————. "Dream Comes True for Amerasian Boy and His Dad." *San Francisco Chronicle,* 2 July 1988.

"Cambodians in Retreat." *Facts on File,* 1–5 January 1979.

Chung, L. A., and Michael McCabe. "Facing the Hopes and Fears of Assimilation. *San Francisco Chronicle,* 25 July 1988.

————. "Bay Area Asians Counting on Economic Success." *San Francisco Chronicle,* 26 July 1988.

Downie, Susan. "Hope and Despair for Cambodians." *San Francisco Chronicle,* 5 July 1988.

Erlanger, Steven. "Missing in Action: From a Lost War, a Haunting Echo That Won't Be Stilled." *New York Times,* 31 August 1988.

Fernandez, Elizabeth. "Amerasian Children Coming Home." *San Francisco Examiner,* 11 October 1987.

Fineman, Mark. "School of Hard Knocks." *San Francisco Chronicle,* 26 June 1988.

Foisie, Jack. "Relations Thawing with Vietnam." *San Francisco Chronicle,* 14 January 1988.

"Hanoi to Aid on Searches." *New York Times,* 31 August 1988.

"Key Opposition to Hanoi–U.S. Ties." *San Francisco Chronicle,* 29 July 1988.

"A Joint Search for MIAs." *San Francisco Examiner,* 31 July 1988.

Johnson, Sally. "Long Road's End for Reunited Asians." *New York Times,* 1 May, 1988.

McLeod, Ramon G. "1965 Immigration Reform Law Opened Door for Asians." *San Francisco Chronicle,* 4 July 1988.

"Panel Votes Aid to Agent Orange Vets." *San Francisco Chronicle,* 30 June 1988.

_____. "McFarlane Believes Some U.S. POWs Are in Indochina." *Wall Street Journal,* 15 October 1985.

_____. "POWs: The Evidence Is There; Now Let's Act." *Wall Street Journal,* 21 April 1986.

_____. "Activists' Bids to Free Any POWs Still in Asia Stir Hopes and Doubts." *Wall Street Journal,* 21 January 1987.

"Payments for Agent Orange Victims" (from Associated Press International). *San Francisco Chronicle,* 6 July 1988.

Roth-Hass, Richard. "Vietnam to Let 50,000 Emigrate," (from United Press International) *San Francisco Examiner,* 17 July 1988.

Teltsch, Kathleen. "Amerasian Influx Expected by U.S." *New York Times,* 9 October 1988.

"U.S. Arms Arrive in Thailand." *Facts on File,* 11 July 1980.

"Vietnam Vets, Chemical Cos. Settle Agent Orange Suit." *Facts on File,* 11 May 1984.

"Veterans Have More Stress Complaints Than Other GIs." *San Francisco Chronicle,* 12 May 1988.

"U.S. Deal on Vietnam's Former Political Prisoners." (from Agence France-Presse) *San Francisco Chronicle,* 16 July 1988.

"Vietnam's Shock." *San Francisco Chronicle,* 18 July 1988.

"Thailand Can't Handle Any More Refugees." *San Francisco Chronicle,* 21 July 1988.

"U.S., Vietnam Set to Hunt MIAs Together" (from *Los Angeles Times*) *San Francisco Chronicle,* 22 July 1988.

"U.S. Not Interested in Talks on Refugees." *San Francisco Chronicle* (from *Los Angeles Times*), 8 July 1988.

"U.S.-Viet MIA Search Due to Begin Soon." *San Francisco Chronicle* (from *New York Times*), 29 July 1988.

"Vietnam Pulls Out of Search for MIAs." *San Francisco Chronicle* (from *Washington Post*), 4 August 1988.

"Vietnamese Refugees Tell of Cannibalism on Boat." *San Francisco Chronicle* (from *Washington Post*), 10 August 1988.

Waters, Rob. "The Ones Who Went 'Home.' " *San Francisco Examiner,* 28 August 1988.

Wedel, Paul. "Vietnam Fires Salvo over American MIAs." *San Francisco Examiner* (from United Press International), 7 August 1988.

Williams, Nick B. "Hanoi Tells of Losses in Cambodia." *San Francisco Chronicle* (from *Los Angeles Times*), 1 July 1988.

"Woman Viet Vet Statue Gets an OK." *San Francisco Chronicle,* 12 May 1988.

INDEX